THE ART *of* BEADWEAVING

Exquisite Beaded Jewellery

Jane Lock

Search Press

A QUARTO BOOK

Copyright © 2013 Quarto plc

Published in 2013 by Search Press Ltd
Wellwood
North Farm Road
Tunbridge Wells
Kent TN2 3DR

ISBN: 978-1-84448-964-0

Conceived, designed and produced by
Quarto Publishing plc
The Old Brewery
6 Blundell Street
London N7 9BH

QUAR: BWJ

Senior editor: Ruth Patrick
Art editor: Jacqueline Palmer
Designer: Tanya Goldsmith
Photographers: Simon Pask, Phil Wilkins
Art director: Caroline Guest
Copy editor: Ruth Patrick
Proofreader: Sarah Hoggett
Indexer: Helen Snaith
Illustrations: Kuo Kang Chen
Picture researcher: Sarah Bell

Creative director: Moira Clinch
Publisher: Paul Carslake

Colour separation in Singapore by PICA Digital Pte. Ltd.
Printed in China by Hung Hing Off-set Printing Co. Ltd.

THE ART

of BEADWEAVING

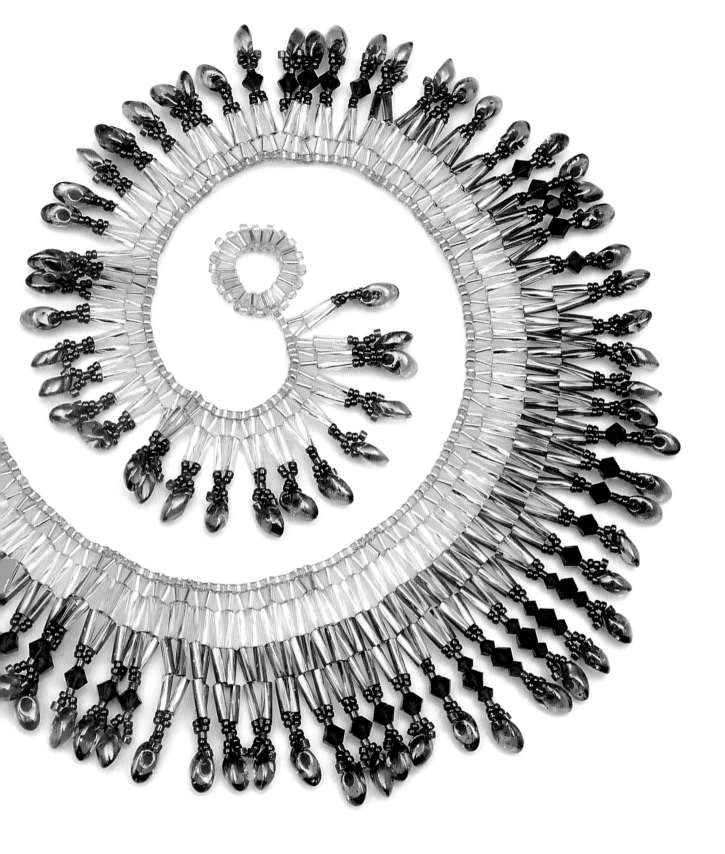

Contents

Foreword

One of my favourite quotes comes from David K. Chatt, who makes exquisite beaded pieces:

'As long as there have been objects with holes in them and people to poke something in that hole, we the people have done exactly that.'

I must warn you, beadweaving is highly addictive. There is a powerful lure in the way chaotic piles of tiny beads can be ordered into lovely, pleasing shapes.

My own introduction to beading was a spiral stitch workshop at my local bead shop about six years ago. After the first inch of spiral rope, I was hooked. I love the slow pace of the craft, that it can't be rushed; you don't need patience, just the capacity to slow down and savour the pleasure of making something beautiful.

By sharing my passion for beading I hope I can set you along your own beading path, introducing you to the main beadweaving techniques to get started and the work of some very fine beadwork designers to spur you onwards.

Happy beading,

Jane Lock

About This Book

GALLERY – PAGES 10–17

To whet the appetite and show just what's possible, a collection of beautiful bracelets, necklaces, rings, cuffs and other examples of beadwork from some of the best designers in the business.

Beautiful photography shows the pieces in detail.

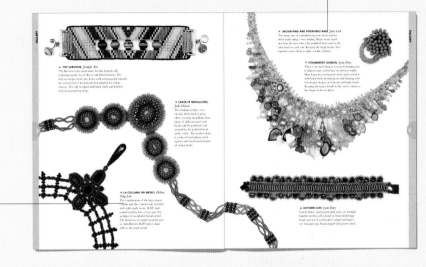

Descriptive captions identify the stitch and beads used in each piece.

CHAPTER ONE – GETTING STARTED, PAGES 18–49

There is rarely a wrong bead, but there is always the right bead for the job. This section shows you how to choose the right tools, thread and beads. Then there's a collection of core techniques, methods you'll use again and again as you work your way through the book, from threading a needle and using a stop bead to attaching a finding and choosing a colour scheme. Finally, there's a troubleshooting section for common problems that even the most experienced beader might encounter.

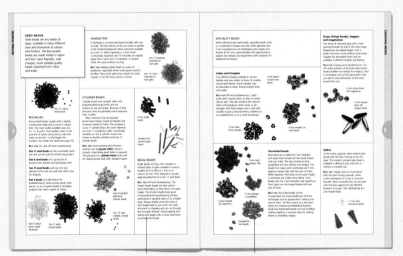

Beads are explored in relation to their size, type and applications.

Photo identifier shows the beads enlarged, so the detail of their shape and finish is evident.

Core techniques are shown with the step-by-step sequences.

Useful tips

Continued overleaf

7

CHAPTER TWO – TECHNIQUES AND PROJECTS, PAGES 50–129

Instructions for beading with seed beads and a needle or on a loom, from the simplest ladder stitch to more intricate netting stitches and beaded beads. The section builds on the basics, with instructions for combining stitches for shapes and texture. All the techniques are illustrated with large-format step-by-step pictures. Throughout this chapter, projects draw on the previous techniques learned and give pattern instructions for making wearable jewellery using the skills you have acquired in the previous section.

For several of the techniques in this section, for each step when new beads are added, the new beads are shown in a contrast colour to the previously added beads for clarity.

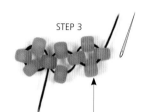

STEP 2

STEP 3

The three new beads added in step 2 are shown in pink.

In step 3, the three new beads added are shown in pink, while the three beads added in previous step are now shown in lilac.

The tools and the types of beads that can be used with this technique and materials are listed.

Finished examples by leading bead jewellery designers show what it is possible to achieve with the stitch.

Actual-size swatches of the stitch worked in a variety of ways show the stitch's potential.

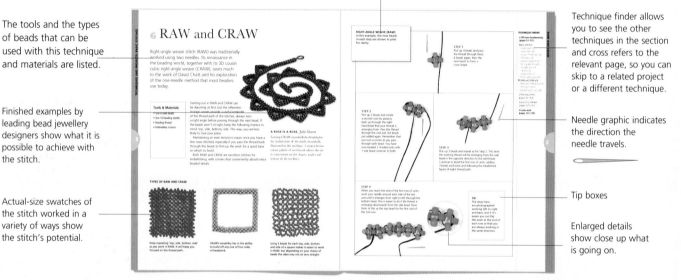

Technique finder allows you to see the other techniques in the section and cross refers to the relevant page, so you can skip to a related project or a different technique.

Needle graphic indicates the direction the needle travels.

Tip boxes

Enlarged details show close up what is going on.

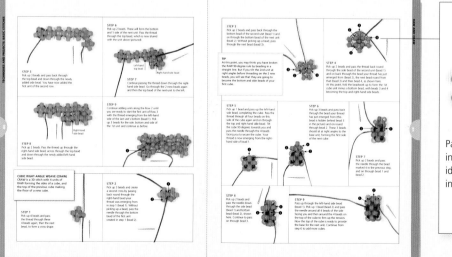

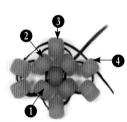

Particular beads referenced in the captions may be identified with a number in a circle.

Tools and materials for the project: quantity, size and type of bead required. Each bead type is accompanied by a graphic that corresponds to the artwork charts. In the tools and materials listing, each bead type is allocated a letter (A, B, C, etc). These letters are referenced in the step-by-step instructions.

Beautiful photograph of the finished project.

Written step-by-step instructions.

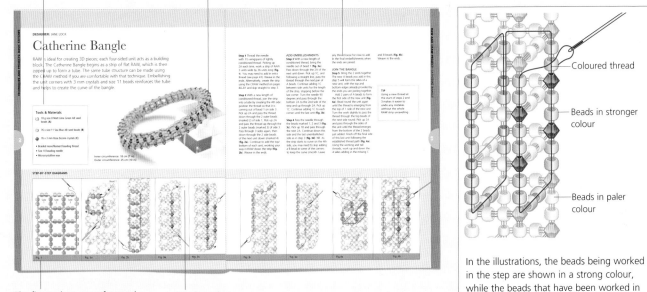

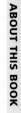

Coloured thread

Beads in stronger colour

Beads in paler colour

The figures here are referenced in the step-by-step instructions.

Numbers that appear on the chart are referenced in the step-by-step instructions.

In the illustrations, the beads being worked in the step are shown in a strong colour, while the beads that have been worked in previous steps are shown in a paler colour. Similarly, the thread path being worked on is shown in a strong colour and the thread path that is complete is paler.

Beautifully photographed example of the finished project.

Plan shows key components referenced in the pattern with identification labels.

Meet the designers – a short introduction to the guest beader.

CHAPTER THREE – GUEST DESIGNER PROJECTS, PAGES 130–151

A chance to put the skills you have learned into practice. This chapter features a wonderful range of projects by internationally acknowledged beading designers. Each project is accompanied by a materials list, including – in some cases – suggestions for bead substitutions in case the exact beads are not available.

Gallery

Showcased on these pages are inspirational examples of work from beaders around the world, demonstrating the beauty and versatility of beadweaving.

▼ **BEADED TREFOIL SECTION NECK CHAIN #1,** *David Poston*
Each three-dimensional oval link in this stainless-steel chain is partially filled with unique seed bead-strung wire, so the necklace looks different from every angle.

◀◀ **BEADED STAINLESS-STEEL WIRE DOUBLE-LINK BANGLE,** *David Poston*
This is a deceptively simple bangle bracelet. The designer has strung seed beads on to wire, then looped them around a welded, stainless-steel frame. But the frame is far from a simple Möbius strip and the beads form a striking palette of complementary blues and greens.

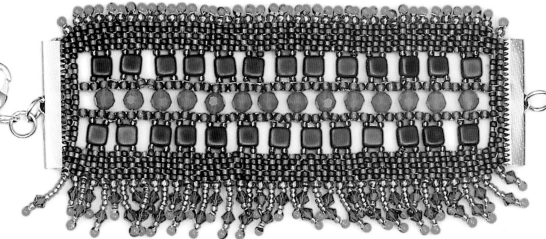

▲ **MISSISSIPPI,** *Caron Reid*

The analogous colours used in this cuff draw the eye away from the two loom work strips towards the strong framework of larger beads in the centre. The edges are embellished with delicate fringes of crystal bicones and drop beads. The bar clasp finishes off the cuff shape nicely.

▲▼ **THREE RINGS,** *Jane Lock*

Simple bands of flat, even-count peyote stitch using size 8 seed beads are dressed up with embellishments: one with a moveable peyote strip of cylinder beads; one with magatamas and size 11 seed beads stitched into the ditches; and the third decorated with a large, lucite flower held in place with loops of size 11 seed beads.

▲ **OODLES,** *Ulli Kaiser*

There is a whole range of techniques featured in this dramatic contemporary necklace, unified by the silver, green and blue colour palette. Strung alongside the silver settings and the semi-precious focal beads are beaded beads using crystal bicones, pompom-style fringed seed beads and beaded crochet.

▲ **'70S SURVIVOR,** *Jennifer Airs*

'70s Survivor is the great name for this loomed cuff,
conjuring up the era of discos and flared trousers. The
chevron stripes in the two loom work sections point towards
the central row of focal beads that inspired the colour
scheme. The cuff is edged with brick stitch and finished
with an unusual bar clasp.

◄ **SANTA FE MEDALLIONS,**
Julie Glasser
This striking necklace uses
circular brick stitch to great
effect, creating medallions from
layers of different-sized seed
beads and fire-polished ovals
around the fire-polished bead
at the centre. The beaded chain
is a mix of herringbone-stitch
squares and intertwined strands
of strung beads.

◄ **LA COLLANA DEI MEDICI,** *Helena
Tang-Lim*
The combination of the big octagon
crystals and the central rivoli, bezelled
with right-angle weave (RAW) and
joined together into a cross, give this
necklace its wonderful historical feel.
The lavish use of small crystal bicones
to embellish the RAW lattice chain
adds to the regal mood.

► **URCHIN RING AND FIREWORKS RING,** *Jane Lock*
Two rings, one of embellished peyote stitch and the
other made using a sieve finding. Bugle beads stand
out from the base with a fire-polished bead used as the
turn bead on each end. Keeping the bugle beads close
together causes them to splay out like a flower.

▼ **STRAWBERRY GARDEN,** *Lynn Davy*
There is no such thing as too much fringing, but
it helps to have a firm base on which to build.
Here Lynn has used peyote stitch and covered it
with brick stitch around pearls and fringing with
Czech glass shapes, seed beads and bugle beads.
Keeping the larger details to the centre enhances
the shape of the necklace.

▲ **AUTUMN CUFF,** *Lynn Davy*
Lovely bronze and peachy-pink tones are brought
together in this cuff; a band of brick-stitch bugle
beads and size 8 seed beads is edged with tiger's
eye semi-precious beads ringed with peyote stitch.

14

◄◄ **SPIRAL STITCH
FLOWERY BRACELET,**
Jane Lock
A straightforward spiral stitch
bracelet using size 8 seed
beads and magatamas in
bright, summery colours is
dressed up with lucite flower
beads added as embellishments.

▲ **AUTUMN CASCADE,** *Jennifer Airs*
The fine inner line of silver-grey beads is
the starting point for this dramatic necklace.
This line of ladder stitch provides the base
for varying lengths of bugle beads to build
up in herringbone stitch.

▼ **DECO SUNRISE,** *Caron Reid*
A loom work cuff using cylinder
beads in lustrous colours. It is edged in
metallic silver using a special technique
incorporated into the design while still
on the loom – a tapestry for the wrist.

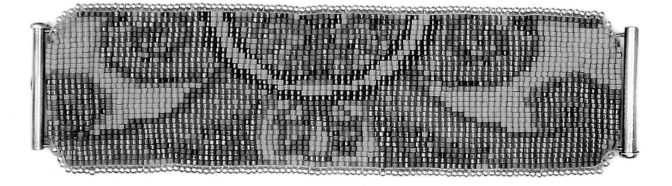

▼ IN A WHILE CROCODILE, *Jennifer Airs*
This is a striking asymmetrical necklace. Beaded beads have been made using even- and odd-count peyote stitch then zipped up into tubes and strung on to beading wire. Glass focal and metal spacer beads emphasise the geometry of the piece.

▼ EASTERN FAN,
Jennifer Airs
Each of the flat blades of this beautiful Japanese-inspired fan is worked in peyote stitch with shaping at the bottom edges. The cascading fringe of seed beads is held together with a herringbone- and peyote-stitch detail, with hidden ladder stitch holding the blades of the fan together.

▲ **BLACK MAGIC,** *Caron Reid*
This is a pared-down version of the
cuff shown on page 11. Using a single
colour shows up the geometric forms
of the central panel of beads between
the two loom work strips and creates
a dramatic mood.

▼ **ASHERAH,** *Joy Poupazis*
This eclectic necklace is a charming
mix of modern and vintage beads
strung together. Adding to the quirkiness
are the strung loops of large seed
beads passing through and around
the bigger beads.

► **LONGEVITY AND LOVE,**
Helena Tang-Lim
Cubic right-angle weave (CRAW) is an
enormously versatile stitch. Here it has
been used to depict a Chinese character,
using short lengths of CRAW beaded off
a longer central piece, with some gentle
shaping for the curves. More CRAW is
used for the rope, interspersed with 'caged'
turquoise beads.

▼ **WARRIOR RINGS,** *Lynn Davy*
This necklace is proof that bezelling doesn't
always have to be around a cabochon or
limited to a few rows. The designer has used
tubular peyote stitch around a large pearl,
building up the layers in circular RAW. The
chain-effect ropes are made from rings of
tubular peyote stitch, again
layered with RAW.

◄ **RUSSIAN SPLENDOUR
NECKLACE,** *Jill Wiseman*
Tubular netting stitch makes
a beautiful beaded rope,
especially when embedded
with fire-polished beads to
show off classic shapes such
as these lovely peyote-stitch
leaves. The leaves have been
joined at the top to form leaf-
shaped pendants that can be
individually removed to vary
the look.

▼ **REGAL SQUARE-STITCH CUFF,** *Jill Wiseman*
Square stitch looks much the same as loom work once
finished, but is a stronger stitch with multiple thread
passes through each bead. Cylinder beads like the ones
used here create a smooth, flexible fabric. The crystal
buttons and bead loop clasps don't distract from the
richness of the contrast colours.

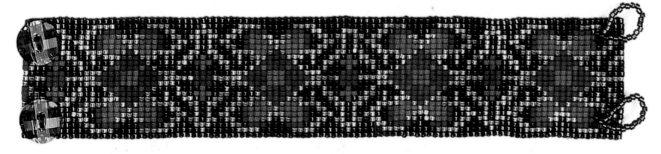

CHAPTER 1
Getting started

This chapter sets you on the beading path with guides
to choosing and using beads, findings, threads and tools.
There is advice on jewellery design and illustrated examples
and tips on working with colour, as well as core techniques
and troubleshooting advice, which will prove invaluable for
making beautiful beadwoven jewellery.

Choosing Beads

Czech fire-polished beads with an AB finish

Crystal beads and drop

Triangles, cubes and cylinder beads

There are only two reasons for choosing a bead: because you have fallen in with love it; or because it will look perfect in the piece of jewellery you are planning or working on. There rarely is a wrong bead, but some beads are more suited to a task than others.

The smallest of beads are referred to as seed beads or rocailles, tiny rounds of glass with large holes designed to take multiple passes of thread. The most uniform-shaped seed beads come from Japan, but the slightly irregular beads from the Czech Republic are highly prized for the variations they offer. Seed beads are the bedrock of beadweaving and it's a good idea to build up a small reserve.

In recent years, seed-bead manufacturers have introduced new shapes; beads such as drops and magatamas work well as 'turn beads' for fringes and picots, while bugles, cubes and triangles of varying sizes can produce pleasing effects in different stitches.

If you want to add sparkle and meaning to your jewellery, crystal beads and semi-precious stones can turn a simple piece of beadwork into an heirloom.

ESTIMATING QUANTITIES

You'll find that the size of beads varies according to manufacturer, finish on the bead and even colour of the bead. This table shows an average approximation of bead sizes and a guide to the number needed to achieve a strung length.

	BEAD (APPROXIMATE SIZE)	BEADS PER 2.5 CM (1 IN)	BEADS PER 46 CM (18 IN)	BEADS PER 61 CM (24 IN)
•	Size 15 seed bead (1.5 mm)	17	307	401
• •	Size 11 seed bead (1.8–2.2 mm)	12–14	210–256	278–339
●	Size 8 seed bead (3.3 mm)	8	140	185
●	Size 6 seed bead (4 mm)	6	115	153
•	2 mm bead	12	230	305
●	3 mm bead	8	154	203
●	4 mm bead	6	115	153
●	5 mm bead	5	92	122
●	6 mm bead	4	77	102
●	8 mm bead	3	57	76
●	10 mm bead	2	46	61
●	12 mm bead	2	38	51

Round seed beads

TABLE OF COMMON SEED BEADS

The table below gives the vital statistics of a number of common bead sizes, providing a conversion chart for the main sizes and the number of beads per gram.

	SEED BEAD SIZE	APPROXIMATE SIZE	NUMBER PER 1 GRAM	NUMBER PER 10 GRAMS	NUMBER PER 100 GRAMS
•	Size 15	1.5 mm	250	2,500	25,000
•	Size 11	1.8–2.2 mm	120	1,200	12,000
•	Size 8	3.3 mm	36	360	3,600
•	Size 6	4 mm	18	180	1,800
	CYLINDER BEAD SIZE	APPROXIMATE SIZE	NUMBER PER 1 GRAM	NUMBER PER 10 GRAMS	NUMBER PER 100 GRAMS
	Size 11	1.6 mm	200	2,000	20,000

Round seed beads with a frosted finish

Rocailles

Cylinder beads

Assorted cylinder and six-sided (hex cut) beads

NAMES AND ABBREVIATIONS OF BEAD COLOURS AND FINISHES

The variety of seed-bead colours and finishes is vast, with a language of its own. Label space means abbreviations are used a lot. Here are the most common ones.

ABBREVIATION	DESCRIPTION
AB	Aurora Borealis. A rainbow effect over the bead colour. On crystals, 2AB means that both ends of the bicone are coated.
Op	Opaque. Solid colours that may also carry another finish.
Trans	Transparent. Clear, coloured glass.
Dyed	A colour applied to glass after the bead is made. While the colours are initially brighter, they can fade over time.
M or Fr	Matt or Frosted. An etched or sandblasted effect that provides a nice contrast when mixed with a shiny finish.
S/L, G/L or C/L	Silver, gold or colour lined. A silver or gold inner coating in a transparent bead, adding sparkle and depth. Colour-lined transparent beads can take on a stained-glass appearance.
Iris	An iridescent effect, similar to that of oil on water.
Metallic	A coating on the glass to make it look like metal. Adds a spot of luxury to a design, but use with caution as the coating can wear off over time. Contact with skin may also affect the coating.

SEED BEADS

Seed beads are tiny beads of glass, available in many different sizes and thousands of colours and finishes. The best-quality beads are made mainly in Japan and the Czech Republic, with cheaper, more variable-quality beads imported from China and India.

CHARLOTTES

A charlotte is a round seed bead (rocaille) with one cut side. The flat surface of the cut creates a sparkle in the finished beadwork. Most commonly available as a size 15, either Japanese or Czech made. Confusingly, Japanese size 15 charlottes are slightly larger than Czech size 15 charlottes, so double check the source before you buy.

BEST FOR Adding subtle detail to a piece of beadwork, especially where small spaces need to be filled. They work well as turn beads for small crystals, or for the final round in a bezel.

Size 15 Japanese charlottes in matt gold

Size 15 Czech charlottes in matt gold

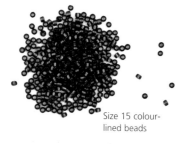

Size 15 colour-lined beads

ROCAILLES

Round seed beads, usually with a slightly curved outer edge and a round or square hole. The most widely available sizes are 15, 11, 8 and 6. The numbers refer to the quantity of beads sitting side by side that make up an inch – so the bigger the number, the smaller the bead (see page 20).

BEST FOR On- and off-loom beadweaving.

Size 11 seed beads are the universally useful size and can be used for almost any project.

Size 8 seed beads are a good size to practise new stitches and techniques with.

Size 15 seed beads work up into very delicate forms and mix well with other sizes for shaping.

Size 6 beads can add texture for embellishments, bead up into quick, bold pieces, or act as spacer beads in stringing projects that need a splash of colour.

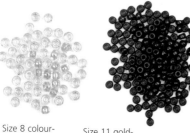

Size 8 colour-lined crystal AB beads

Size 11 gold-lustred beads

CYLINDER BEADS

Cylinder beads have straight sides with proportionately large holes and are uniform in size and shape. Because of their precision, they are generally more expensive than rocailles.

Often referred to by the popular brand name Delicas (made by Miyuki) and Treasures (made by Toho). The standard is a size 11 cylinder bead, the same diameter as a size 11 rocaille but taller. Increasingly available are size 8 cylinder beads (also known as double cylinders) and size 15 cylinder beads.

BEST FOR Loom weaving and off-loom stitches such as **peyote stitch**, where a smooth, close-fitting bead fabric is required. The precision of a **cylinder bead** works well for making bezels and other beaded shapes.

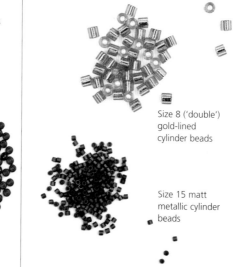

Size 8 ('double') gold-lined cylinder beads

Size 15 matt metallic cylinder beads

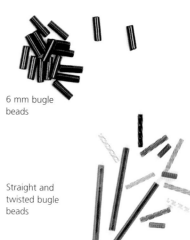

6 mm bugle beads

Straight and twisted bugle beads

BUGLE BEADS

Bugle beads are long, thin, straight or twisted tubes of glass available in various lengths from as little as 2 mm to as long as 24 mm. Their diameter is usually approximately that of a size 11 seed bead.

BEST FOR Off-loom beadweaving. The longer length bugles are best used in bead embroidery, as they tend to be quite fragile. The shorter lengths look good incorporated into beadweaving stitches, particularly in spiralled ropes or as a ladder base. Always double check the ends of each bugle bead as you work; the ends are prone to chipping and can cut through the strongest threads. Trying topping and tailing each bugle with a round seed bead to protect the thread.

SPECIALITY BEADS

While still technically seed beads, speciality beads come in a multitude of shapes and sizes. Both Japanese and Czech manufacturers are developing new shapes and finishes all the time, giving beaders the opportunity to explore new designs and experiment with variations for traditional techniques.

Cubes and triangles

Two different shapes available in various finishes and sizes similar to those of rocailles (round seed beads). Some triangles may be described as sharp, having straight sides and angles.

BEST FOR Off-loom beadweaving. Cubes work well in square stitch, as they sit neatly side by side. They also enhance the chevron effect of herringbone stitch nicely, as do triangles. Both bead shapes mix in well with rocailles to give a textured effect, whether as an embellishment or as a small focal bead.

4 mm green-lustred cube beads

5 mm silver-lined triangles

4 mm metallic iris cube beads

Drops (fringe beads), daggers and magatamas

Tiny drops of coloured glass with a hole passing through the top of the drop shape. Magatamas are slightly bigger, with a larger hole and a more bulbous drop shape. Daggers are elongated drops and are available in different lengths and finishes.

BEST FOR Fringing and embellishments. The off-centre position of the hole makes these beads excellent turn beads for fringing. Used in techniques such as flat spiral stitch, they can add an extra dimension to the loops around the core.

4 mm colour-lined AB magatamas

5 mm opaque black AB dagger beads

Two-holed beads

Manufacturers in both the Czech Republic and Japan have introduced new bead shapes with two holes. This has created exciting possibilities for new stitches and designs. Tila beads from Japan and Czechmates are 5 mm (approx.) square tiles with two sets of holes. While Japanese Tila beads can be quite fragile, Czechmates are a little more robust. Twin Beads from the Czech Republic and SuperDuos from Japan are rice-shaped beads with two sets of holes.

BEST FOR Two-holed beads can be incorporated into many traditional off-loom techniques such as square stitch, netting and peyote stitch. The flat surface on a tile bead allows for interesting embellished features, while two-holed seed beads can link modified netting together in unusual ways for making flower or medallion shapes.

5 mm matt opaque Tilas

6 mm opaque CzechMates

Crystal metallic AB SuperDuos

Transparent Twin beads

Spikes

As the name suggests, spike-shaped glass beads with the hole running across the base. This modern, pressed glass bead is available in different sizes and with or without a rounded top.

BEST FOR Usually used as a focal bead with the point facing upwards, either as the centrepiece of a ring or around a bracelet. More unusually they can be used with the base uppermost (see Nefertiti Necklace on page 138), highlighting the coin-shaped base.

17 mm clear and green spikes

CRYSTAL BEADS

The term 'crystal' is correctly applied to any glass bead with a lead content, giving the glass added weight and sparkle. There is some debate about the safety of crystal beads, with manufacturers reassuring beaders that the lead is sufficiently bound in with the glass mix to prevent any harmful exposure to the skin. Any potential risk would only come from ingestion in substantial quantities and for that reason it is recommended that crystal beads are not used in jewellery intended for small children.

CRYSTAL BICONES

Both Swarovski from Austria and Preciosa from the Czech Republic produce fine crystal bicone beads that add sparkle and glamour to any beadwork. Like two pyramids joined at the base, a bicone can range in size from 2.5 mm up to 12 mm, from something as small as a seed bead to a 'diamond' as big as the Ritz. The cut sides or faceting enhances the sparkly quality of the crystal. Inexpensive Chinese crystals are increasingly available, but can be of variable quality.

BEST FOR The smaller bicones combine well with seed beads for weighty, luxurious-looking beadwork, while the larger sizes make spectacular focal beads. The range of sizes makes them good for projects such as beaded beads, when two or three sizes of the same bead may be required. Crystal has sharp edges, so use braided thread such as Fireline or Wildfire.

6 mm AB
Swarovski crystal

6 mm opal- and
plain-coloured
Swarovski crystal

6 mm opal
Chinese crystal

CZECH PRESSED GLASS SHAPES

The traditional manufacturing technique of pressing molten glass into a mould allows for almost any shape to be recreated in glass, with fine details picked out on the surface of the bead.

BEST FOR The vast range of shapes available makes pressed glass beads perfect for focal beads, especially if there is a theme to the design – leaves, flowers, shells and so on. A centre-drilled flower shape makes a pretty bead clasp, as used in the Cubist Cuff project on page 56.

Pressed glass
leaves and bell
flowers

COATED CRYSTAL PEARLS

Crystal beads especially coated with a lustred finish to reflect the beauty of a natural pearl and combine it with the uniformity of a manufactured bead. Glass pearls are an inexpensive alternative. Like the real thing, the lustre can wear off if too much friction is placed on the finish. The size range is similar to that of the crystal bicones.

BEST FOR Any design that needs the uniformity of a manufactured bead to work but benefits from the lovely pearlised finish – for example, beaded beads take on a historical feel when using crystal pearls.

4 mm Swarovski
pearls

CZECH FIRE-POLISHED GLASS

Often included in the crystal category because these faceted beads work well as an inexpensive alternative to crystals, but they are, in fact, lead free. The faceted beads are reheated after manufacture to melt and soften the edges of the cut sides and to give a gleam to the glass. Available sizes range from 3 mm to 12 mm and the rounded shape is similar, though not identical, to the proportions of a crystal bicone.

Best for Although often considered an economical substitute for crystal, fire-polished glass has a weight and warmth of its own. The sparkle may not be as flashy as crystal, but the beads work well where any variety of size is needed for a project or where small jewels look good embedded within a piece of beadwork.

4 mm, 6 mm, 8 mm and 10 mm fire-polished beads

4 mm and 6 mm beads in the same colour, although the 6 mm looks darker

4 mm fire-polished beads with plain and coated finishes

6 mm silver-coated fire-polished beads

RIVOLIS

A rivoli in the beading world describes a round cabochon (bead with no hole) with a faceted front and back rising to a low point. The back is often foiled. The best-quality rivolis tend to be those from Austria and the Czech Republic.

Best for Centrepieces on necklaces, earrings and bracelets. Because rivolis have no holes, they need a bezel to hold them in place. Adding to and embellishing those bezels with more crystal and metallic seed beads can turn a crystal bezel into an heirloom jewel. Look at La Collana Dei Medici on page 12 for a perfect example.

18 mm, 12 mm and 14 mm rivolis

SEMI-PRECIOUS BEADS

The world of semi-precious stones is a fascinating one; so many stones with different scientific properties and folkloric properties associated with magic, astrology and therapeutic qualities. Using natural stones in beadwork can add meaning and value to a design. Whether or not you subscribe to the values associated with a semi-precious bead, featuring a birthstone in a gift is a special gesture.

Various sizes of peridot tumble chips

TUMBLE CHIPS

Tiny chips of semi-precious stone. Semi-precious stones, as the name implies, can be expensive, but these little chips are an affordable way of buying a bit of natural luxury. The quality of tumble chips does vary and the drilled holes can vary a lot in size and position.

Best for These small chips are perfect for incorporating into bead woven designs such as the Spiral Necklace on page 96 or using as embellishments and fringing. The irregular shapes add an organic, natural feel to any project.

Choosing Findings

Findings are the small pieces of metal that help build a piece of jewellery and hold it all together. Often in beadweaving you can work on several projects without ever having to use a finding and I am happiest when I can finish a necklace or bracelet without a metal clasp, but sometimes they are unavoidable and they can make a good piece of jewellery perfect.

The metals used in findings can vary from base metal to solid gold – the first clue is always the price. The most commonplace finishes are silver- or gold-plated nickel-free base metal or copper. My favourite metal is sterling silver; beadweaving is not a hurried craft and it seems only right to finish off your hard work with a good-quality finding (where practical, of course). A length of sterling-silver chain is a serious investment, but a pair of sterling ear wires not only adds value to your work, it limits the risk of sensitivity.

EARRING FINDINGS

It is a good idea to keep an assortment of earring findings to hand. Look out for original shapes online and at local craft fairs. Earring findings are available in a variety of finished base metal and sterling silver. Sensitivity can be a particular issue for earrings, so always go for the best-quality metal you can afford.

Types

Ear wires come in various styles, most commonly fish hook shaped, with twist or ball details. If you're comfortable with wirework, making your own shapes is a great way to add extra flair.
BEST FOR Dramatic drop earrings.

Ear posts, also known as studs are held in place with a butterfly back. The front might be flat, ready for the decorative element to be glued on, or with a small loop from which to hang a focal bead or beadwork.
BEST FOR Small drop earrings.

Lever backs, sometimes called continental ear wires, have a small, hinged latch that holds the earring securely in place.
BEST FOR Heavier designs, since the lever holds the earring in place.

Hoops can be worn as they are, but where is the fun in that? Use the hoop as a base for brick-stitch work or to thread beads on to. Some have additional loops for chandelier-style earrings.
BEST FOR These can make a great base for beadwork, particularly brick stitch.

Clip-on and screw-on earring fittings are designed for non-pierced ears. I find the clip-on fitting more comfortable to wear than the screw-on version, but it depends on your personal preference.
BEST FOR Clip-on fittings work well for lightweight designs; screw-on fittings are more secure, but can be uncomfortable if fixed too tightly to the ear.

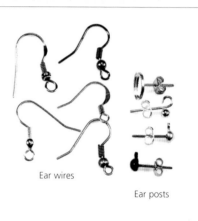

Ear wires

Ear posts

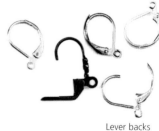

Lever backs

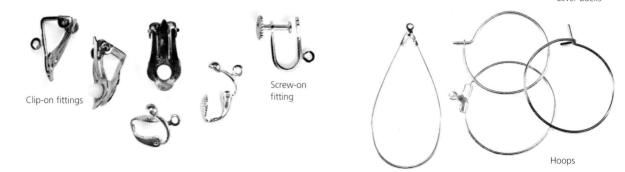

Clip-on fittings

Screw-on fitting

Hoops

JUMP RINGS

Jump rings are unsoldered metal rings that join items together. Open and close using one or two pairs of chain-nose pliers. The larger the jump ring, the easier it is for one to come apart – so always try to go for the smallest size you can work with.

Types

Round 3–8 mm diameter 3 and 4 mm diameters are the most useful sizes to have around. Available in silver and gold plate, antiqued silver, gold, copper and bronze finishes. Sterling silver, gold filled (a thick layer of gold plating) are more expensive.
Best for Joining clasps to necklace or bracelet ends; joining lengths of chain together or beads to chain or ear wires. Slipping a jump ring through a seed bead can be a quick way to join a piece of beadwork to an ear wire or clasp. Take care not to break the bead when using this technique.

Jump rings

SPLIT RINGS

Split rings are like tiny key rings, making them more secure than jump rings, but they can be a bit fiddly to open. Join a loop or closed ring by levering one side of the split ring up and slipping in and twisting the new ring underneath.

Types

Round 4–5 mm are the most useful sizes in beadwork. The range of finishes is smaller than that of jump rings, usually including gold- and silver-plated and sterling silver.
Best for Use a 4 or 5 mm split ring as the other half of a lobster or bolt clasp. Unlike a jump ring, it can't open accidentally.

5 mm split rings

Joined split rings

CRIMPS

Tiny, yet powerful, rounds of soft metal. They squash flat or fold to hold wires, tigertail and beads in place.

Types

Round crimps are slightly shorter than they are round. Use with chain-nose pliers.
Best for Use with one or more strands of wire or tigertail to finish a piece of strung jewellery.

2 mm round crimps

Tube crimps are designed to be used with crimping pliers, as they fold over without snapping.
Best for Unlike round crimps, tube crimps will fold without breaking. Use with crimping pliers around two strands of wire or tigertail to give a professional finish.

Tube crimps

Crimp covers curve around a flattened crimp and, once closed, look like a bead. Use chain-nose pliers or the front section of a pair of crimping pliers to close them into a ball around the crimp.
Best for Giving a professional finish.

Crimp covers

CALOTTES

Also known as necklace ends or clamshells. Calottes wrap over a crimp to hide it and to provide a place to attach the clasp. Some calottes have a ready-made loop to the top or side; others need the loop finishing with a pair of round-nose pliers.

Types

2–5 mm sizes in various plated finishes and sterling silver.
Best for Necklaces without too much weight.

Assorted calotte styles and finishes

Coil cord ends

CORD AND RIBBON ENDS

These operate in a similar fashion to calottes, but sometimes need the addition of glue to hold everything in place.

Types

Cord ends There are different styles to choose from, but they all work in much the same way: fold each side down over the cord and then crimp firmly with a pair of chain-nose pliers. Use jump rings to attach clasps to cord ends.
BEST FOR Cord ends allow you to turn any length or style of cord into a necklace from which to hang a pendant.

Ribbon ends Available in different lengths and finishes.
BEST FOR Wider ribbon lengths keep their shape when used with a ribbon end. You can use ribbon ends to finish off a strip of beadwork, but take care not to squash any beads as you attach it.

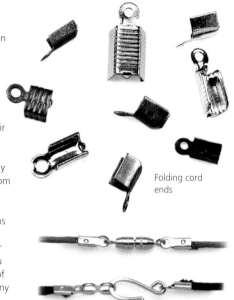

Folding cord ends

Cord ends with toggle clasps

Cord ends with barrel and hook clasps

CHAIN

Joined links of plated metal or sterling silver used to hang pendants or can be decorative pieces in their own right.

Types

Curb and trace chains are the standard styles and are usually sold in unit lengths ranging from 1 cm (½ in) to 1 m (1 yd). Check the length as well as the price of a unit when buying to avoid costly mistakes. Available in silver and gold plate, antiqued silver, gold, copper and bronze finishes, or sterling silver.
BEST FOR As a quick alternative to a beaded chain for a bracelet or necklace. Short lengths work as extension or safety chains. A short chain added to an ear wire and bead makes a quick, dramatic earring.

Curb chain

Trace chain

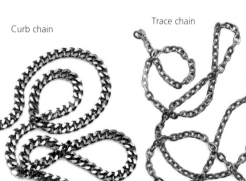

HEAD PINS AND EYE PINS

Head pins are lengths of metal wire with a small ball or flat end to prevent beads from falling off. Eye pins are much the same, but with a loop from which to hang other beads.

Types

Head pins Available in lengths from 1 cm (½ in) to 10 cm (4 in). Some head pins come with decorative ends.
BEST FOR Head pins are the findings you need to turn beads into pendants or earring drops.

Eye pins Available in lengths from 1 cm (½ in) to 10 cm (4 in). Available in silver and gold plate, antiqued silver, gold, copper and bronze finishes, and sterling silver.
BEST FOR As well as being used for turning beads into pendants or earring drops, eye pins can be joined together to form a beaded linked chain.

Eye pins

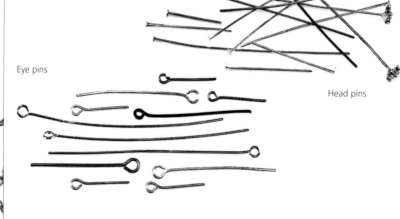

Head pins

CLASPS

Beaded clasps are not always the answer, so it is worth getting to know the metal finding options available.

Types

Toggle Usually a ring with a T-bar clasp. Also available in many different shapes.
Best for Bracelets. A toggle clasp won't easily slip undone. Remember to check that the bead at the T-bar end is small enough to slip through the ring.

Barrel A barrel clasp is shaped like a long barrel, with two halves that screw together. Use the best quality you can find, as ill-fitting halves can twist undone too easily. Also known as a screw or torpedo clasp.
Best for A traditional style for knotted necklaces. Not a good choice for bracelets, because they are impossible to do up with one hand.

Lobster clasp One of the most popular styles of clasp; the little lever catch needs a split ring or soldered jump ring to complete the fastening. An ordinary jump ring tends to come undone. Available in many different sizes and finishes. Choose the right one for your design.
Best for A standard clasp for bracelets and necklaces, but join to a beaded bead with a head pin and a jump ring and you have a handbag charm.

Bolt ring Like a lobster clasp, the bolt ring uses a split ring to join the ends of a bracelet or necklace together. Available in many different sizes and finishes. Choose the right one for your design.
Best for The simplest and most discreet form of clasp. An extension chain at the other end can be easier to do up.

Magnetic clasps are the easiest to use – just place the two ends close to each other and they will pop together. Being magnetic, they are attracted to other metal, so use with a safety chain on bracelets. The two halves usually form a round shape when attached, but keep an eye out for other styles.
Best for Magnetic clasps are popular for less nimble fingers, but always check with the recipient before using them as they are not suitable for people with pacemakers.

Sliders A slider clasp has two bars of metal, one hollow and the other solid. The former slides over the latter. They are available in various lengths. Sometimes magnetised, slider clasps come with two, three, four or five loops.
Best for Multi-stranded bracelets and necklaces – they hold their shape better with a slider clasp.

Toggle clasps

Barrel clasps

Lobster clasps

Bolt ring clasps

Bolt rings

Magnetic clasps

Sliders

29

Threads

Choosing the right thread depends on several factors: the type of beads you are using, whether the finished beadwork will be worn or admired from afar, and your personal preferences. There is no point in struggling on with a thread you have been told is ideal if you hate using it, so use this section as a general guide and feel free to bend some of the rules if that works better for you.

Beading threads in general owe a lot to fishing. You will often find that tigertail beading wire and bonded threads have a weight test number on the spool. This refers to the weight of fish the line will carry, not the weight of a necklace it can bear. Beading threads are usually nylon or the stronger but less-flexible braided monofilament threads. Both are used with beading needles. Beading wires, generically known as tigertail, are stiff enough not to require a needle and are what you would use to string a necklace of individual beads, such as the Beaded Bead Necklace on page 108.

THE WINGSPAN EXPLAINED

Many patterns, including the projects in this book, refer to a length of thread as a wingspan. Stretch out both your arms as if you were trying to fly; that's your wingspan. Now do it again, unreeling the thread between your hands as you do so. Stop unreeling just before you get to the full wingspan and, taking a firm grip of the thread, stretch it out the rest of the way.

Read the label

The major brands of tigertail have a label displaying the wire's diameter, colour and number of strands. Higher stranded, flexible tigertails are more expensive. The break weight will be greater on thicker tigertails, which refers to the wire's origin as a fishing line.

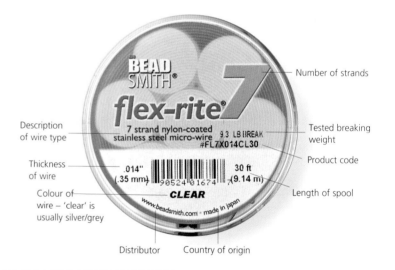

Number of strands

Description of wire type

Thickness of wire

Colour of wire – 'clear' is usually silver/grey

Tested breaking weight

Product code

Length of spool

Distributor

Country of origin

THREAD COLOURS

The different brands of nylon thread are available in a wide variety of colours, some offering a wider selection than others. All the major brands will include black, white, cream and natural shades. For most beadweaving stitches, a neutral colour is all you need.

NYLON

Nylon thread is the mainstay of beadweaving. Every experienced beader has a different favourite brand. Some are less inclined to fray or knot, others might have a little more stretch, but all brands benefit from stretching and conditioning (see pages 33 and 42) before you start beading.

Brands and colours

S-Lon (Superlon) Available in a wide range of colours.
KO Available in a limited range of colours.
Nymo Available in a wide range of colours.
BEST FOR Loom work, off-loom designs that need a flexible drape and/or a close colour match to the beads. Avoid using nylon thread to attach metal findings, since it can quickly wear through.

S-Lon thread

KO thread

BRAIDED MONOFILAMENTS

These threads have no stretch and rarely fray, but it is still a good idea to condition them to prevent knots and to help with tension. Sizes are mostly described by weight. Available in 0.1 mm (4 lb) and 0.12 mm (6 lb). 0.12 mm works for most projects.

Brands and colours

Fireline Crystal (white) and Smoke (it's a good idea to pass Smoke through a paper towel to remove the excess colour before you start beading).
Wildfire Available in green, black and frost.
PowerPro Available in white, moss green, bright yellow and red.
BEST FOR Off-loom stitches, especially those incorporating crystals, bugles and semi-precious stones with sharp edges. The beaded fabric is generally inflexible, making it useful for 3D shapes and beaded beads (see page 104).

Smoke Fireline thread

TIGERTAIL

Stranded, nylon-coated, stainless-steel wire. 7 strands is standard, rising to 49 strands for ultimate flexibility. Thicknesses range from 0.25 mm to 0.6 mm and weight strengths from 10 to 40 lb (if you want to go fishing). Cut from the reel, with flush cutters, not scissors.

Brands and colours

Flex-rite Available in a wide range of colours.
Beadalon Metallic colours, including sterling silver.

Acculon Available in a limited range of colours.
Soft Flex Available in a wide range of colours, including sterling silver.
BEST FOR Stringing beads, finishing with crimps and clasps. While 0.46 mm 7-strand tigertail is good for most stringing projects, highly flexible 49-strand tigertail such as Softflex creates a fibre-like drape while benefiting from that steel core. Great for stringing sharper-edged semi-precious stones and crystals.

Softflex

7-strand tigertail

ELASTIC

Stretchy, versatile, stronger than you'd think and child friendly. Ranging from 0.5 mm to 1.8 mm diameters.

Brands and colours

Stretch magic Available in a limited range of colours.
Elasticity Available in a limited range of colours.
BEST FOR Simple bracelets finished with a knot or a crimp. 0.5 and 0.7 mm diameter elastic will even take size 11 cylinder beads, opening up all sorts of possibilities for unisex bracelets in favourite or team colours.

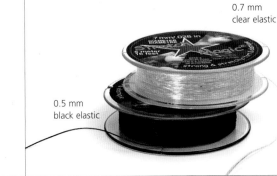

0.7 mm clear elastic

0.5 mm black elastic

Tools

When you first start out in beading, it's perfectly okay to raid the toolbox for pliers and cutters. But once you get the beadwork bug, you will find it so much easier and more enjoyable to have the right tools for the task.

The beadweaver's basic tool kit is not enormous, leaving you more to invest in the beads themselves. As your skills advance, experience will encourage you towards better-quality and more specialist tools. If you develop a passion for loom work, some of your requirements will differ from those of the off-loom beadweaver, not least your investment in a loom. Like most things, the rule of thumb for investing in quality is to pay as much as you can afford at the time.

Basic Off-loom Beadweaving Kit

These three basic items, along with beads and thread, are all you need to start beadweaving.

• Bead mat
• Beading needles
• Embroidery scissors

Basic Loom Beadweaving Kit

In addition to the loom and beads, you will need these basic items to start beadweaving on the loom.

• Bead mat
• Beading needles
• Embroidery scissors
• Ruler
• Masking tape

BEADING NEEDLES

Very fine, flexible needles designed for beading through small seed beads. Japanese and English needles are the most expensive and some beaders swear by them; Indian needles, although the cheapest, are fine to start with. All needles eventually bend, and sometimes even break. Keep a few bent needles nearby – they can be useful for getting round tight corners.

Types

Regular The different sizes (see below) refer to the needle's thickness and the size to choose will depend on the size of bead your thread needs to pass through.
Shorts (sharps) The shorter length means less needle to bend, so these work well for beading through fabric (bead embroidery).
BEST FOR
Size 10 Size 8 seed beads and larger.
Size 12 Size 11 seed beads and larger.
Size 13 Size 15 seed beads and smaller.

Beaded wooden needle case

BEAD MATS

Made from a fleece-like fabric. The lighter-coloured mats are better to work on – unless you are using clear or very pale colour beads, in which case have a darker shade to hand. A bead mat holds all the beads in place as you work with them. Put a mat on a tray so you don't have to tidy everything away each time you need to reclaim the table. Stick the beading needle into it to make it easier to find, pick up and keep safe. The mats are machine washable.

Bead mats

Types

Bead mats are available in various colours and are generally one size (35 x 28 cm/14 x 11 in). The fabric is easily cut to fit trays or the lids of storage boxes for beading on the move.
BEST FOR Everything, but especially off-loom beadweaving. The mat fabric stops beads from rolling around and keeps them in place when you are trying to pick one up with a needle.

THREAD CONDITIONER

Always try to use thread conditioner on any beadweaving thread to reduce tangling, knotting and fraying. The waxy finish also gives some waterproofing protection to the nylon threads.

Types

Thread Heaven Was developed specifically for all types of needlework, but is particularly popular among beaders for conditioning nylon and braided monofilament threads.
BEST FOR The petroleum-based wax helps to prevent the build-up of static electricity and so reduces the risk of tangles.

Beeswax You may prefer a natural product for conditioning thread and beeswax is a readily available material. Avoid using candle wax, even in a beading emergency; additives such as perfume will ultimately damage the thread.
BEST FOR Natural beeswax is an inexpensive conditioner that provides thread with a protective, non-slip coating.

Artificial or microcrystalline wax is a manmade wax made to mimic beeswax, but without the same tendency to break down over time. Like beeswax It creates friction on the thread, allowing the beader to work with a tight tension.
BEST FOR Microcrystalline wax works well with braided monofilament threads. It has a lower melt temperature than beeswax and can be gently rinsed off with warm water (as long as your thread is waterproof!).

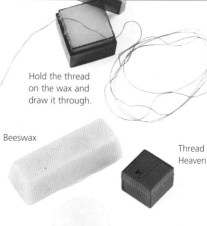

Hold the thread on the wax and draw it through.

Beeswax

Thread Heaven

Microcrystalline wax

LOOMS

Bead looms vary from the basic, tabletop wire frame to free-standing, wooden-framed looms. Looms vary hugely in size and function so knowing which one to choose first can be daunting. The safest option is to start with a simple, horizontal wire-framed loom that is often sold as a child's toy. We've used it in this book to demonstrate the techniques and the bookmark project on page 129 was made on one.

If you catch the loom work bug, you may want to upgrade after a few projects. Your budget will be the major consideration, but after that think about the largest project you are likely to take on. Many looms (even this basic one) have adjustable rollers that allow longer pieces to be made, but the width is constant.

A horizontal tabletop loom (with the warps parallel to the work surface) is practical for tidying away, but a vertical loom that can sit on your lap brings the beadwork closer, with less strain on your back and neck. Just don't make any sudden movements.

Larger, free-standing looms are often adjustable in height and width to suit the size of the project.

Types

Wire-frame looms are the most basic and most bead stores will carry them (sometimes in the children's section). They are lightweight but sturdy enough for small projects such as bracelets or the bookmark on page 129. Available in tabletop models.
BEST FOR Starting out on. Wire-frame looms are compact and easily stored. Usually under $15 and complete with instructions and everything you need to try the technique out.

Wooden-frame looms come in many styles across a wide price range. Available with fixed or adjustable frames, in upright and tabletop models.
BEST FOR Adjustable frames allow you to work on larger projects. Upright looms are the more complex, giving more flexibility and requiring greater loom skills.

33

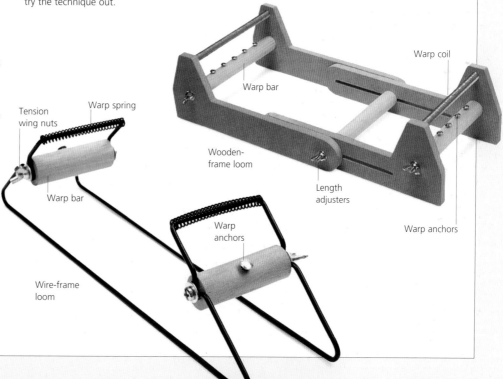

Warp coil

Warp bar

Wooden-frame loom

Length adjusters

Warp anchors

Tension wing nuts

Warp spring

Warp bar

Warp anchors

Wire-frame loom

CUTTERS AND SCISSORS

There are a lot of different cutting tools designed for specific threads and wires. Using the right tool will prolong the life of the blade to keep giving clean cuts and save on frustration.

Types

Cutting pliers are designed to be used with wires, head pins and metal-based threads such as tigertail. Side and flex cutters are the most useful for beaders. **BEST FOR** Side cutters will cut head pins, tigertail and thinner wires. Keep the straight side facing the edge you are cutting. Save your flex cutters for getting a clean cut on tigertail.

Scissors Having both sharp embroidery scissors and a pair of craft scissors to hand will save both time and stress.
BEST FOR Small embroidery scissors are very sharp and ideal for cutting the nylon threads such as Nymo or KO. Fireline and similar threads wreck embroidery scissors, but a pair of inexpensive craft scissors works perfectly.

Side cutters

Embroidery scissors

PLIERS

Pliers are primarily used for wirework, but if you want to make earrings, pendants or chain-based jewellery with your beadwork, you will need at least two pairs. When choosing chain-nose pliers, make sure you get smooth jaws or the metal will mark. The more expensive box-joint pliers will last longer than those constructed with a lap joint.

Types

Chain-nose pliers are available as straight or bent-nose. The straight pliers are sometimes incorrectly referred to as flat-nose pliers.
BEST FOR Opening and closing jump rings, gripping head pins and squashing crimps. Bent-nose pliers are more specialist, but can be useful for getting between beads. Don't use either type for pulling stuck needles through beads unless you absolutely have to.

Round-nose pliers have two round graduated 'blades', designed for making rings and loops in wire.
BEST FOR Making loops in wire and head pins, and finishing off the loop on a calotte.

Crimping pliers For folding a tube crimp into a neat band.
BEST FOR They take a little practice to get used to but give a professional finish to your beadwork.

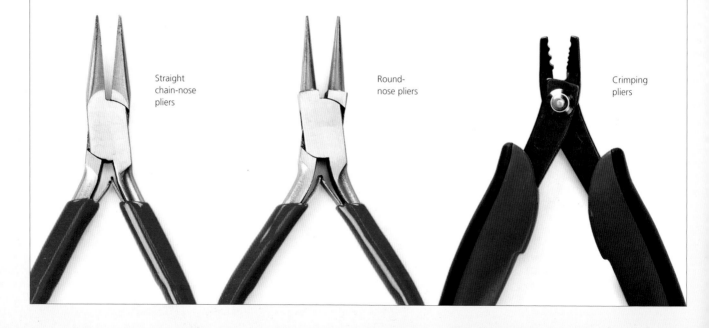

Straight chain-nose pliers

Round-nose pliers

Crimping pliers

OTHER USEFUL TOOLS

Bead scoop (or teaspoon) A bead scoop comes in handy for rounding up piles of seed beads back into their bags and tubes, but a teaspoon can work just as well.

Bead trays are useful ceramic dishes with sections to keep beads separated and easy to pick up with the needle. Watercolour artists also use them as paint palettes.

Thread Zapper gently melts the ends of thread to prevent fraying.

Ruler, tape measure and gauge You sometimes need to take measurements: a length of beadwork, the size of a wrist or the diameter of a bead. A ruler is also useful when following charts, as it will allow you to keep track of the row you are working on.

Masking tape You can use small pieces of masking tape instead of tying knots in the thread to attach ends to the loom (see Weaving on the loom, step 1, page 125).

Sizers These basic necklace and bracelet EZ sizers are good for double-checking lengths of a strand as they take the diameter of the beads into account. The necklace sizer helps to work out the design on multi-stranded necklaces. By joining the two sides of the flat semicircle, you get a tube with various lengths marked off. Drop on a finished bracelet or necklace to read the final length or use masking tape to fix unfinished strands to the sizer to work out the positions of each strand.

Bead boards have curved grooves with centimetres and inches marked off and sections for holding beads and findings. The boards are useful for planning the layout of a necklace or bracelet.

Bead board (actual size: 30 x 23 cm/12 x 9 in)

Bead tray

Bead scoop and tray

Bead scoop

Ruler

Bead gauge

Tape measure

Bracelet sizer

Thread Zapper

Masking tape

35

Workspace and Storage

With a craft as addictive and absorbing as beading, it is easy to forget your surroundings. But where you bead and how you sit while beading can affect your wellbeing as well as your creativity, so it is important to stay as comfortable and organised as possible.

First, decide on a space in which to bead. It doesn't have to be a whole room; it can be a desk and some shelves, or even a tray on the kitchen table that can be tidied away in a hurry. It does have to be comfortable and well lit; the chair and work surface need to be at the right height, and make sure there is directional lighting to reduce the strain on your eyes. Take regular breaks and move about, have your glasses to hand if you wear them and most importantly, stay relaxed.

Find a safe place to store your beads, away from bright sunlight and extremes of heat. A shelf, a cupboard or a toy chest into which you can tidy away lidded and compartmentalised boxes or stacking jars is ideal. If your beading space has to multi-task, it is best to keep everything in clear containers so that you can easily find what you need.

Stacking jars
Crystals can chip each other if kept loose. Store them in bags or lidded containers to reduce tarnishing and to avoid the silver being confused with the base metals.

STORING OLD BEADING NEEDLES
I keep bent and broken needles in a plastic mints container. Sometimes you need a bent needle to get into an awkward spot; you are also keeping them safely away from children and pets. Check with your local services provider when it comes to throwing away old needles.

Storage options
Assorted tubes and divided flip-top storage boxes keep beads and findings safe from spillages and discolouration. Clear plastic is best, since you need to be able to see what's inside.

36

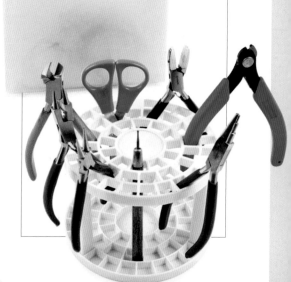

MONEY-SAVING STORAGE IDEAS

There is a wide choice of storage available, but it doesn't have to be exclusively designed for beading or be expensive. Craft storage in general is easily adapted to suit a beader's needs. Keep an eye out for fishing tackle or hardware storage options as well. Tool and tackle boxes are often designed to be carried around. Office supplies such as desk tidies and pen pots make excellent homes for pliers and other tools. Ring binders and magazine boxes can all be put to good use by the beader.

Best of all, recycle and upcycle; reuse cleaned, lidded food-storage containers, and repurpose sealable sandwich bags. I've seen an empty box of chocolates lined with a bead mat function perfectly as a mobile work tray – though it might be kinder to your fellow beaders to cover the lid to avoid raising their hopes of a sweet treat!

37

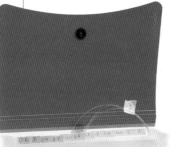

Hardware storage

Hardware and tool storage often comes with handles, and lidded and compartmentalised containers, making it ideal for beads, tools and threads.

Storing seed beads

Keep seed beads in the bags or tubes in which they are sold with the label attached, making it easier to remember the name of colour or the supplier.

Storing threads

One good storage method is to thread your bobbins on to a large stitch holder usually used in knitting. This will keep them together and help to avoid them unravelling and getting tangled.

Design and Colour

As you delve deeper into the art of beading, you will find yourself wondering, 'What would happen if I changed this... or that?' My advice is always to try it and see; the joy of beading is that if anything doesn't work you can always reuse the beads.

COLOUR

Choosing colours can feel like the hardest part of designing beadwork. Part personal taste, part matching an outfit or occasion, it is easy to feel overwhelmed by all the possible combinations.

Working with colour comes easily to some people, while others have to work harder to find the right mix. It helps to start with one colour and add to it shade by shade until the palette looks just right. There are tools and sources of inspiration that can help if you get stuck – but remember, if you like the colours then they are the right colours.

THOUGHTS TO CONSIDER

- Who are you making the beadwork for and when will they wear it? A bracelet for a surfer dude is going to need to withstand constant wear and exposure to the elements. Naturally waterproofed threads such as a braided monofilament, combined with matt beads, will withstand greater wear and tear and appeal more to the sporty type.

- A bride's necklace might be worn just once, but it needs to shine almost as much as she does. Create the dramatic sparkle with crystals, sterling silver and pearls.

- Think of a necklace as having three parts: a front section and two side sections.

- All three parts will be identical if you're beading a rope, but when it comes to adding detail, symmetry works best; a focal bead or beaded pendant that sits at the centre of a necklace keeps the piece well balanced. Try to work with odd numbers of beads

or components so that there is a centre to work your design around.

- Chunky jewellery makes a grand statement, but remember to take the weight of large-scale beadwork into consideration. A big, bold necklace is easier to wear if the central section is hung from lengths of ribbon making up some of the side sections, rather than being beaded all the way around the neck.

- A delicate necklace will hang better if there is a focal point at the front.

- On a bracelet, too large a single element will unbalance the whole piece. Spacing a few focal details around the wrist will look great and be more fun to wear.

- Mixing simple elements together with ornate components draws the eye to the focal point of the piece of jewellery. Lots of simple elements repeated create a structural, modern effect.

Colour wheels

A colour wheel will help guide you through the world of primary, secondary, analogous, complementary and contrasting colours. Pick your main colour and turn the wheel to find other shades to blend around it.

Primary colours
The primary colours red, yellow and blue cannot be made by mixing any other colour.

Secondary colours
The secondary colours are orange, green and purple and are made by mixing red and yellow (orange), yellow and blue (green) and blue and red (purple).

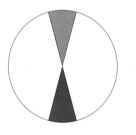

Complementary colours
Complementary colours face each other on the colour wheel, saying nice things to each other. They can be equally strong so mix with some analogous colours to soften the scheme or leave as they are for a striking, contemporary feel. The pairs of complementary colours are orange/blue, violet/green and red/green.

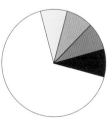

Analogous colours
Analogous colours sit side by side on the colour wheel; sometimes referred to as a tone-on-tone colour scheme, analogous colours can soften a single bolt of bright colour and create a sense of movement.

38

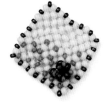

This rivoli-centred flower was the result of doodling with peyote-stitch leaf shapes.

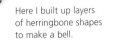

Here I built up layers of herringbone shapes to make a bell.

I've played with other ideas such as stitching in the ditch on a strip of peyote stitch to create waves.

PLANNING A PIECE

Get used to keeping a notebook close to hand. Even if you can't draw, just writing down a few words around a scribbled picture can capture the design idea well enough for you to refer back to.

Never give up on an idea; learning new techniques can unlock an old inspiration, unleashing a fresh approach.

Try doodling with the beads themselves. Beading a swatch and folding it, embellishing it or adding different elements, can help to trigger an idea. With some techniques such as square or peyote stitches, you can paint pictures and designs within the fabric of the beadwork.

Charted patterns are easy to draw up and all you need is some graph paper; better still, look out for graphing software programs such as Bead Tool that will help you with finished sizing, bead quantities and even transforming a photograph into a beaded picture.

If you've been asked to make a specific item for someone, ask them to show you pictures of what they have in mind. Show them jewellery you have already made, then discuss the style, length, weight and function of the new piece so that you are both thinking along the same lines.

Here I combined peyote and herringbone stitches to make a strange yellow and orange flower.

Doodling with beads

Try doodling with beads – in the same way as you might doodle with a pen on paper while on the phone; you may be surprised by the creative results.

ETHICAL BEADING

Beadwork designers are generally a relaxed bunch, but copying a design, published or otherwise, and passing it off as your own design can generate some ill will, if not an actual lawsuit. When you publically share a piece of beadwork made from a book, magazine or tutorial, give the original designer credit. If you want to teach another designer's tutorial, you should seek their permission first. Never copy a purchased pattern to pass on – you will be infringing the copyright of the designer or magazine.

We all take inspiration from the work of others – that's how most of us learn and grow as beaders – but if you want to promote or sell a piece made from another's design, check the original designer's policy first. These days, blogs and social media make it easy to get in touch and you will usually receive a friendly, helpful response.

These earrings were inspired by Sabine Lippert's Volcanoes Necklace. Sabine's way of beading around the centre bead was so satisfying I just had to try joining them together.

BEAD SOUP

Pour colour-related oddments of various-sized beads into a bowl and see what sort of a soup you get. It is a fun way to introduce some randomness into your beadwork and it may suggest pleasing combinations you might not otherwise have thought of. Make up a band of peyote or brick stitch with the mix and see where it leads you. See Lynn Davy's Freeform Cuff on page 60.

I've used mostly size 11 beads, with a dash of 4 mm crystals and a splash of 5 mm triangles in this bead soup to make a different version of the Loop the Loop Bracelet on page 120.

COLOUR SCHEMES IN ACTION

Seeing colour schemes in action is the best way to understand how to mix and match different shades. The more you play with colour combinations, the more you will discover for yourself.

Tones of summer

This summer-inspired necklace by Lynn Davy uses a monochromatic pink palette subtly interspersed with cream and tones from either side of the pink spectrum on the colour wheel. The splashes of analogous colour help to bring out the fine detail of the fringing and the textures of the pearls and pressed-glass beads.

Colours of the rainbow

Natasha VanPelt's necklace makes a clever use of bright, analogous colours. The rainbow of colour through the curve of fringing creates a lively sense of movement and the bright green of the base and rope holds the design together visually as well as practically.

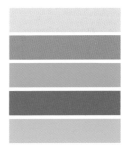

Cool-spectrum, analogous scheme

This necklace features an analogous colour scheme containing just blues and greens, from the cool part of the colour wheel. While the asymmetric shape of the collar is unusual, the colours are soothing and soften the otherwise strong geometry of the beaded shapes. This necklace is by designer Jennifer Airs.

Perfectly complementary

The main colours in Jill Wiseman's bangle are perfectly complementary. Orange and turquoise face each other on the colour wheel and the finish on the metallic beads subtly hints at a potentially bright colour palette. The matt brown, an analogous colour to the orange, sits in the background to emphasise the contrasting colours rather than overwhelming them.

PICKING A COLOUR PALETTE

All this talk of colour schemes and wheels can be daunting. Simplify your first steps by taking a favourite object or item of clothing for your inspiration.

My paisley scarf, received as a gift one year, falls a long way outside my colour comfort zone and the combination of burgundy, green and turquoise colours would not have occurred to me had I not needed a piece of jewellery to complement it. At first glance, these colours don't fit the colour wheel rules. But look again: the greens, the burgundy, and the neutral creamy orange all add up to a split-complementary colour scheme, enhanced with the analogous pink and turquoise tones to add depth. The bracelet pattern is less detailed than the scarf, so I picked out the main colours and left out the supplementary ones without losing the overall effect.

Don't worry, it really isn't necessary to analyse every colour palette; sometimes a pleasing combination just works.

Core Techniques

While preparing your needle and thread is obviously core to successful beadweaving, there are a few basic jewellery-making techniques that are also handy to know. Adding metal clasps to tigertail and beadwork as well as a making a simple beaded loop for a focal bead are just a few of the ways to finish off your beadwork.

THREADING YOUR NEEDLE
One of the hardest tricks to learn when beginning beading is how to thread those small-eyed needles.

STEP 1
Bringing your thread to the eye of your needle is a difficult method to use, as it gives the thread a chance to slip around either side of the needle rather than go through the eye. The trick is to bring the needle to the thread instead.

STEP 3
Bring the eye of your needle down to the thread and push it on to the thread. This gives the thread the only option of going through the eye. As soon as a piece of the thread is through you can continue pushing, or pull the rest of the thread through.

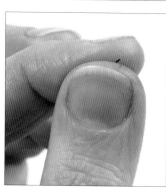

STEP 2
Hold your thread with the sharply cut end sitting between your thumb and index finger on your non-dominant hand – you want to hold it so you can barely see it. The more you can see of it, the more it is able to move and the harder it will be to thread.

TIP
Make sure the end of your thread has a sharp, clean cut to help you to thread your needle.

STRETCHING YOUR THREAD
When your thread comes off the reel it will be still coiled, making it much more likely to tangle together and get knotted. The cure for this is to stretch it. Pull the thread with your hands with sufficient force to straighten it. You'll find it is now a lot easier to work with.

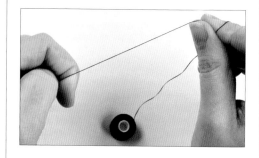

USING A STOP BEAD
A stop bead is one threaded on at the start of your work to help with your tension as well as to stop your beads from falling off your thread. Simply pick up one bead, slide it towards the end of your thread, and circle back through it a few times, ensuring you don't split your thread. You need to thread through it enough times so that it doesn't easily slide, but not so many that it will be hard to remove at the end of your work.

ADDING A NEW THREAD

A quick method for adding and finishing threads is to use a slip knot. It works best if you use the end of the thread that comes off the reel first – you may find it easier to keep track of this by not cutting your new thread until you have joined it to the old one. Stop beading while you have at least 20 cm (8 in) of the old, working thread left and leave the needle threaded on.

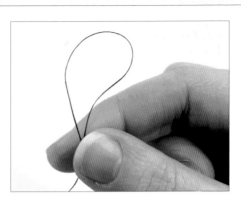

STEP 1

Make a loop near the end of the new thread, with the long length lying on top.

STEP 2

Place your index fingers through the thread loop and, taking hold of the long length of thread, pull it through the loop.

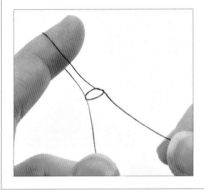

STEP 3

You will be left with a loop that you can adjust or loosen depending on which thread end you pull.

STEP 4

Place the end of your old thread end through the new loop and pull on the new thread to tighten the loop. Weave the old thread back down through the beadwork. Continue beading for a few rows, then weave the tail of the new thread through them to secure as before.

CRIMPING

When working with threading materials such as tigertail, you will need to learn how to crimp the ends of your work to attach a clasp. The Beaded Bead Necklace on page 108 uses this technique.

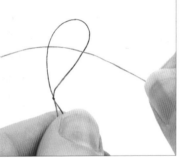

STEP 1

Cut a length of beading wire, allowing 3–4 cm (1¼–1½ in) extra at each end to attach the clasp, using wire cutters or heavy-duty scissors – good scissors will be spoiled by the wire. Thread on your beads. Thread a crimp on one end of the wire, then thread the wire through the clasp.

STEP 2

Thread the beading wire back through the crimp, leaving a loop that allows movement but looks neat.

STEP 3

Now flatten the crimp with crimping pliers or chain-nose pliers. Slide the beads up to meet the crimp, passing them over the loose end of the thread if possible; if not, cut the loose end very close to the crimp, then slide back the beads. Add another crimp to the other end of the wire and attach the other end of the clasp as before, allowing for some movement but without the thread showing too much.

TIP

Use two crimps if you have heavy beads.

CALOTTES

The more flexible varieties of tigertail can be knotted at the ends, or between beads. These can be attached to the clasp using a calotte over the knot at the end of the strand. This is also a simple way to attach several strands of beads to a clasp.

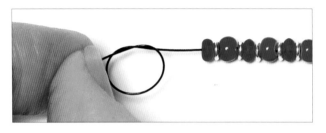

STEP 1

Cut a length of beading wire, allowing 4–5 cm (1½–2 in) extra at each end to attach the clasp, using wire cutters. Thread on your beads. You may want to anchor one side of your work to the work surface with tape while you finish the other. Make an overhand knot in the other end of the wire.

STEP 2

Place the knot into a calotte and use chain-nose pliers to gently squeeze it over the knot.

Look for the little groove in the calotte for the thread to sit in.

STEP 3

At the other end, make an overhand knot and put a blunt needle into it. Use the needle to slide the knot close, but not too close, to the beads. Squeeze another calotte over this knot.

STEP 4

Depending on the type of clasp you are using, it can either be attached to the calotte by opening the loops on the clasp, or by gently opening the loop on the calotte, with pliers. Then clip off the ends of the beading wire.

CALOTTES ON A MULTI-STRAND NECKLACE

A calotte works well over one or two crimps to join several strands together in a necklace or bracelet. This technique is used on the Beaded Bead Necklace (see page 108).

STEP 1

Use two crimps to attach the strands of the necklace or bracelet together. Clip the ends of the threads, then put a calotte around them.

Squeeze firmly, but not so hard that the threads are damaged.

STEP 2

Squeeze the calotte together with chain-nose pliers. Close it firmly enough to hold the strands in place without shearing them. Repeat on the other side and attach a clasp.

FINISHING MULTI-STRANDS INTO A CONE

A cone end or a large coiled cord end (see page 28) is a stylish way to hide several wires when there are too many to fit through one calotte.

STEP 1

Make your strands of beads and check that they will hang together well by holding them up. Use calottes to secure the ends, making small loops at the end of each thread (see page 43).

STEP 2

Cut two new lengths of beading wire and make a simple loop at the end of each one. Gather the strands of beads, threading through the loops on each strand. Thread back into the new loops.

STEP 3

Now put a cone at each end of the necklace over all of the ends of the strands.

Check again to see how the strands hang together.

STEP 4

Thread more beads on to each of the single threads and crimp them on to a clasp.

BAR CLASPS

These clasps are great for cuff bracelets and choker necklaces, because they are long and thin and keep wider sections of beadwork flat and in place. The Ribbons and Rows Bracelet on page 132 shows another method of adding a bar clasp.

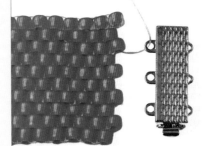

STEP 1

Place the bar clasp alongside the finished edge of the beadwork, aligning the beads to the clasp fixing points. Bring the needle out through one of the beads nearest to one of the fixing points on the clasp. Pass the needle through the corresponding fixing point on the clasp.

STEP 2

Thread the needle back through the bead in the main body of the beadwork. Repeat once or twice more until it feels secure.

STEP 3

Repeat in the same way for the other fixing points on the clasp. Attach the other side of the clasp to the other end of the beadwork in the same way.

BEAD AND LOOP CLASPS

Bead and loop clasps are a very popular way of finishing off pieces of jewellery. They are one of the most discreet clasps, because they can be constructed from the same beads used in the necklace or bracelet, making them an integral part of the piece. A similar method is used for the Loop the Loop Bracelet and would work well on a loomed bracelet, too.

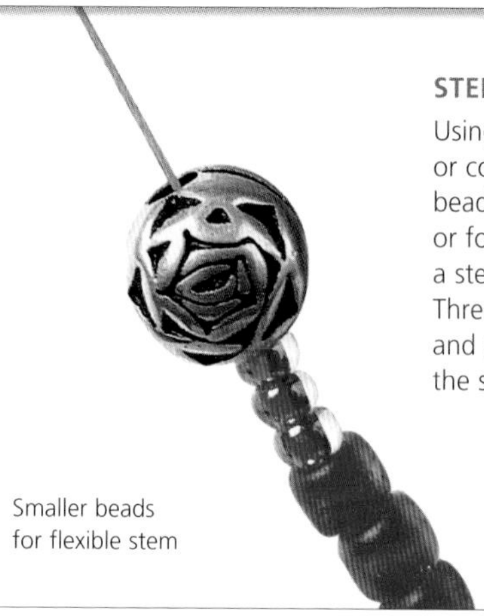

STEP 1

Using a colour that matches or complements the main beadwork, thread on three or four seed beads to form a stem for the focal bead. Thread on the focal bead and push it down towards the seed beads.

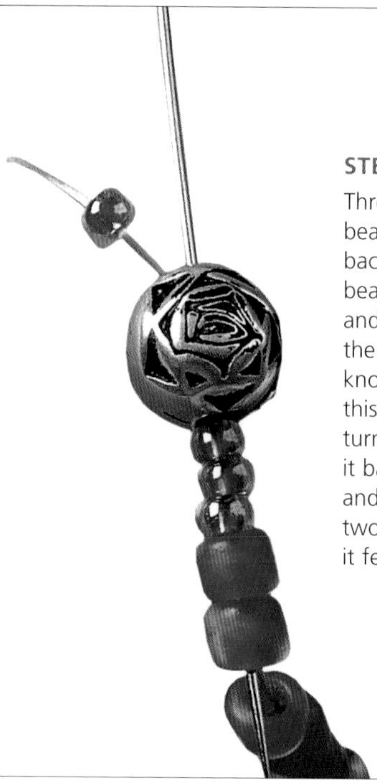

Smaller beads for flexible stem

STEP 2

Thread on another seed bead, then take the needle back down through the focal bead, the three seed beads and into the main body of the beadwork. Tie a single knot between two beads at this point to allow you to turn the needle and thread it back up through the beads and around the focal bead two or three more times until it feels secure.

STEP 3

Add a stem of three or four seed beads at the other end of the beadwork. Thread on more beads to make a loop large enough to slip over the focal bead at the opposite end.

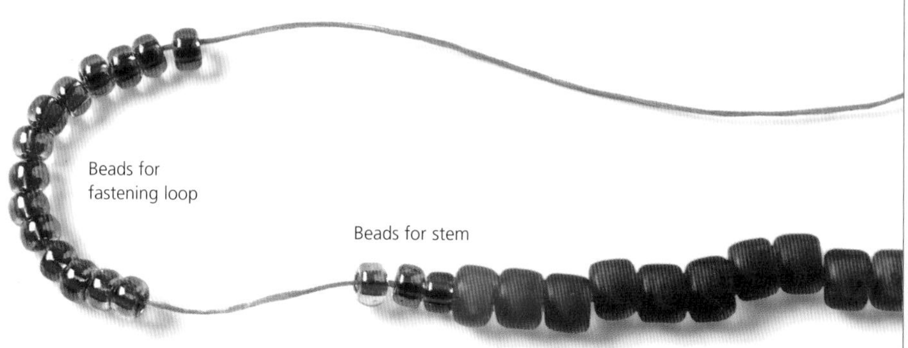

Beads for fastening loop

Beads for stem

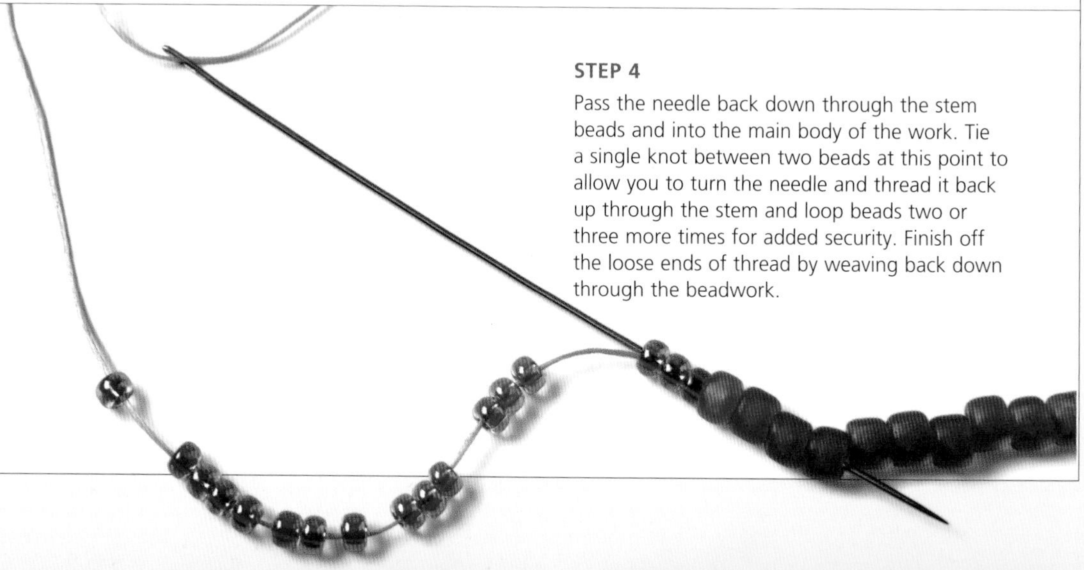

STEP 4

Pass the needle back down through the stem beads and into the main body of the work. Tie a single knot between two beads at this point to allow you to turn the needle and thread it back up through the stem and loop beads two or three more times for added security. Finish off the loose ends of thread by weaving back down through the beadwork.

TOGGLE CLASPS

A toggle clasp consists of a ring and a T-bar with a looped fixing point on each one. Always remember to add a stem of a few small seed beads at each end of the beadwork to make it easier to pass the T-bar through the ring. This method will only work if the fixing point of the clasp is closed. The thread will slip through a jump ring.

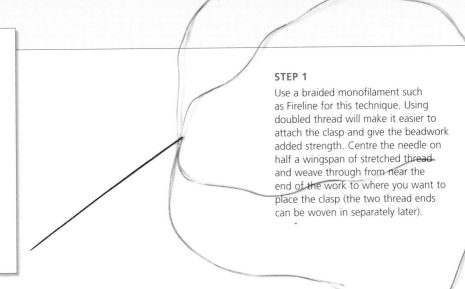

STEP 1

Use a braided monofilament such as Fireline for this technique. Using doubled thread will make it easier to attach the clasp and give the beadwork added strength. Centre the needle on half a wingspan of stretched thread and weave through from near the end of the work to where you want to place the clasp (the two thread ends can be woven in separately later).

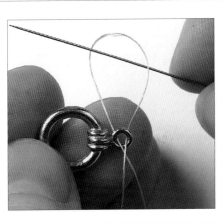

STEP 2A

Take the needle through the fixing point on the ring section of the clasp, leaving a loop of thread on the other side. Secure the thread by passing the needle through the loop.

STEP 2B

Pull the doubled thread firmly to secure it to the ring.

Use smaller beads at the end for a flexible stem

STEP 3

With a new half wingspan of thread, repeat steps 1–2B for the opposite end.

CLASPS IN ACTION

A number of the projects in this book use bead and loop clasps, including the Friendship Bracelet (see page 70), the Loop the Loop Bracelet (see page 120) and the Rosetta Bracelet (see page 142).

Experiment with different focal beads and loop beads in your designs.

The Friendship Bracelet uses a 6 mm bicone crystal as the focal bead and size 11 seed beads as the loop beads.

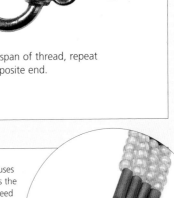

Troubleshooting

The simplest way to recover from a beady mistake is to say, 'It's supposed to be like that.' This approach is fine if you forget to step up in tubular herringbone, but won't do if a broken thread threatens to destroy your precious beadwork. These pages will help you identify what can be fixed and how to fix it.

KNOTTED THREAD

Stretching and conditioning the thread helps to reduce the risk of knots in the wrong place (see page 42). But they still occur. Try keeping your beadweaving movement smooth and calm – this way, you can spot a knot before it is too tight to unravel. Do not pick at a knot with the needle; this just frays the thread. If you can't unpick the knot with your nails or fingers, then you will have to cut the thread and unpick the work until you have a long enough tail to add in a new thread.

ONE BEAD TOO MANY?

You may spot an extra bead in an earlier row, or a beaded toggle may be too tight to fit over a bar or focal bead. Carefully try to break the extra bead by pinching it between the tips of a pair of chain-nose pliers. Cup your hand over the bead to avoid shards of flying glass and take care not to break the thread. Ease the remaining beads around the gap to help the beadwork sit better. In this example, we added an extra bead into two different peyote-stitch rows and broke out the second bead. Can you spot where it was?

READING CHARTS

Finding and keeping your place on a chart is easier if you keep a ruler under the row you are working on. Charts written for square stitch or loom work are the simplest to follow, because the graph, like the stitch, is built in straight lines. Pick up one bead at a time in square stitch and one row of beads at a time on the loom.

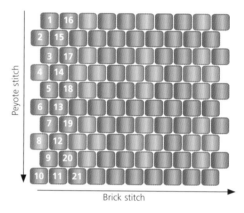

The numbered beads show the order in which they are picked up for a peyote-stitch pattern in two colours, illustrating the offset thread path.

Peyote-stitch charts can be more confusing to follow, so it does help to be comfortable with the stich's thread path before you tackle one. The beads are offset in each 'row' so you zigzag between the beads you pick up and the beads you pass the thread through. To begin with, you pick up the beads for the first two rows.

Brick-stitch charts can look the same as peyote-stitch charts but are read at a 90-degree angle. For example, in the chart above for peyote stitch, read the chart from bead 1 at the top left and follow the numbered beads. For brick stich, start with a ladder-stitch base at beads 10, 11 and 21 to the end of the row and build up the horizontal rows from there. Each chart will usually indicate the starting point and direction of work.

BENT NEEDLE AND BROKEN NEEDLES

Bent needles are an unavoidable problem that can be turned to your advantage; save them for pulling thread through tight spots such as when weaving the ends back through a bezelled rivoli (see page 99).

If the needle bends too far it can break, breaking the thread in the process. If this happens, you need to undo your work a few rows until you have enough working thread to attach to a new thread.

CULLING BEADS

Misshapen or broken seed beads are a fact of the beadweaver's life. It is a good idea to weed out or 'cull' the faulty beads before you start a project, to avoid problems halfway through. Some bead shapes such as bugle beads are more prone to chipped ends than others and need extra care when culling.

UNPICKING YOUR WORK

If you spot a mistake that you can't put up with or that throws the counting out, it can save time and tempers in the long run to simply stop and unpick the work.

Unthread the needle first and gently pull the thread back through, one bead at a time. Do not try passing the needle back the way it came or you might split the thread and make the situation worse.

UNRAVELLING BEADWORK THREADS

Despite of your best efforts a thread can sometimes start to unravel, especially if the beadwork has been worn a few times. Adding in a half-hitch knot here and there when you weave the ends back in can help to prevent this. To create a half-hitch knot, catch the needle under a thread between two beads. Pass the needle back through the loop created and pull firmly.

Adding a dab of clear nail varnish to the end of the thread also helps to hold it in place. Don't use glue if you can avoid it, as this is irreversible.

Always try to use a new thread for sewing on the clasps. That way, if they do start to come loose you can replace them without having to unravel the body of the work itself.

If unravelling does occur in the beadwork, prepare a needle with a new length of thread (approx. 30 cm/12 in) and leaving at least a 15-cm (6-in) tail, follow the stitches' thread path, and 'darn' a patch at least 2.5 cm (1 in) either side of the loose thread. Finish off by weaving the two ends in.

If the threads have unravelled so much that beads are coming adrift, it may be possible to stitch them back in, depending on the original stitch. In this example, the thread on the outer row of a brick-stitch swatch came undone, losing one bead. To repair it, unravel the thread until there is a long enough tail to weave back in. Prepare a new needle and thread and, using brick stitch, replace the missing beads. Weave all the ends in to secure.

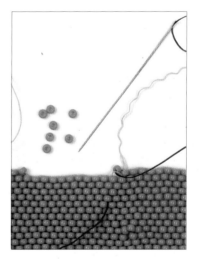

CHAPTER 2

Techniques and projects

This is the part of the book you have been waiting for; step-by-step instructions for popular beadweaving techniques, with accompanying projects to put your newly acquired skills into practice. These techniques lay a path to exciting stitch variations and combinations to prepare you for tackling the guest designers' projects in Chapter 3, and moving on to other beading adventures.

1 Ladder Stitch

At first glance, the varied design possibilities of ladder stitch are not immediately obvious, but don't let its apparent limitations fool you. Several popular beadweaving techniques depend on it; both herringbone and brick stitch usually begin with a ladder-stitch base, and in brick stitch it's a great way to quickly increase beads at the beginning or end of a row.

Tools & Materials

- Size 8 seed beads
- Size 10 beading needle
- Beading thread
- Embroidery scissors
- Stop bead

A very simple ring can be made using ladder stitch and bugle beads. Just measure around your finger to work out the length you'll need. Strips of ladder stitch work as loops for closures, as well as being the foundation of other stitches.

Because the stitch requires the beads to sit side by side, it can seem quite fiddly at first, and (as you will see by the photographs) it is almost impossible to get round-sided beads to sit comfortably next to each other. Weaving back through the beads will usually sort out any stragglers, as well as strengthening the strip. If a straight line is vital, use either bugle beads or even cylinder beads.

PAGAN NECKLACE, *Jennifer Airs*

An unusual interpretation of ladder stitch; elements made from bugle beads of different lengths are ladder stitched together and the threads disguised by clever strands of seed beads finished off with picots.

TYPES OF LADDER STITCH

Stacks of size 8 seed beads can be quickly joined together to make a simple wristband. Don't get over-ambitious, though, since too many round-sided beads in a stack will be difficult to control.

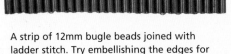

A strip of 12mm bugle beads joined with ladder stitch. Try embellishing the edges for a simple bracelet.

Ladder stitch stacks of 6 mm bugle beads topped and tailed with size 8 seed beads together for an exaggerated ladder effect.

LADDER STITCH

Size 8 seed beads are used here, but you can use bugle or cube beads to get started if you find that easier.

STEP 1

Thread the stop bead and pick up 2 beads. Position the beads so that they sit side by side.

Stop bead

STEP 2

Pass the needle back up through the first bead added.

STEP 3

Pass the needle back down through bead 2. Tighten the thread so that the 2 beads are held comfortably side by side. The tension is loose in the picture so that you can see the thread path.

STEP 4

Pick up a bead, and pass the needle back down through bead 2, keeping the tension even so that the beads sit side by side.

STEP 5

Pass the needle back up through bead 3.

STEP 6

Continue to add further beads by following the figure-of-eight thread path through each bead. The tension needs to be firm enough to keep the beads side by side, but not so tight that they are pulled in towards one another.

2 Square Stitch

I have always suspected that square stitch was invented by a disgruntled loom weaver who couldn't face threading up another loom. I have no historical evidence to support this theory, only the fact that the stitch creates a near-perfect facsimile of loomed beadwork without having to set up the warp threads.

Tools & Materials

- Size 8 seed beads
- Size 10 beading needle
- Beading thread
- Embroidery scissors
- Stop bead

CITY WINDOWS EARRING AND RETRO NECKLACE, *Michelle Hamill*

These little flags of coloured and silver cylinder beads are perfect for showing off how effective it is to bead small areas of decorative colour with square stitch.

This time-saving detail makes square stitch ideal for creating smaller items using loom patterns. Any charted pattern for loom work or indeed for knitting or cross stitch also provides great source material, though these may need adjusting for the various bead shapes.

The multiple passes of thread through each bead (up to four) make it a very strong stitch as well as being useful with different or assorted bead shapes in one piece of beadwoven fabric.

Bear in mind that those same multiple passes also make it quite a tricky stitch to unpick. A firm tension is ideal, though be cautious when mixing bead shapes and avoid pulling the work out of shape.

Square stitch works well with cube beads; everything sits so beautifully together, making it a good place to start with the stitch. There are two start methods for square stitch, shown on the following page.

TYPES OF SQUARE STITCH

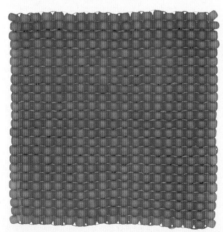

Plain square stitch made using size 8 seed beads gives a strong and flat beaded fabric that won't easily come undone.

Square stitch is good for using charted patterns. Size 8 beads were used here, but for more detailed patterns use smaller beads.

Combining square stitch with other techniques can make different shapes. Here vertical strips of square stitch made with Method 2 are joined by two rows of ladder stitch to make a frame.

METHOD 1

In this example, the new beads in each step are shown in lime green for clarity.

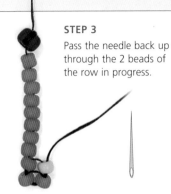
Stop bead

STEP 1

Thread the stop bead and pick up the required number of beads. Pick up 1 more bead (lime bead) and position it side by side with the last bead threaded. Pass the needle down through this last bead and back up through the new bead.

STEP 2

Pick up a bead and position it on top of the previous bead and side by side with the bead parallel to it. Pass the needle down through 2 beads in the previous row.

STEP 3

Pass the needle back up through the 2 beads of the row in progress.

STEP 4

Repeat steps 2 and 3 for each bead added, passing down through 2 beads of the previous vertical row and up through the 2 beads of the row in progress. Continue to work rows up and down, from left to right, until the piece is as long as required. I find it easier to turn the work so that I am always working 'up' the row.

METHOD 2

You can use the first three steps of this method to make a slinky beaded rope as an alternative to chain (see page 103).

STEP 1

Follow steps 1 and 2 for ladder stitch (see page 53) to join 2 beads together.

STEP 2

Pick up 2 beads and pass the needle down through the left-hand bead of step 1 (bead 1), and back up through the right-hand bead and new bead above.

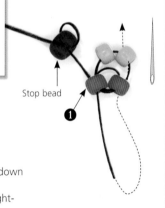
Stop bead
❶

STEP 3

Pick up 2 beads and repeat step 2 until you have a strip of the required length.

STEP 4

Turn the strip so that your thread is now coming out of the top right-hand bead (your stop bead will also be on the right).

STEP 5

Continue adding 1 bead at a time as in step 1 for Method 1, turning the work if you prefer to work 'up' the row. For this third row and beyond, the thread passes through 2 beads of the previous row. For a more flexible weave, pass the thread through one bead only (as in the project on the next page).

DESIGNER: JANE LOCK

Length: 19.5 cm (7¾ in)
Width: 3.5 cm (1⅜ in)

Cubist Cuff

A straightforward technique like square stitch doesn't have to produce straightforward jewellery. Here we've mixed beads of different shapes and finishes, even allowing the thread colour to show through one bead to enhance the overall colour. Because of square stitch's similarity to loom work, it adapts well to following a chart.

Tools & Materials

- 147 x 4 mm Czech fire-polished beads Light Topaz (**A**)
- 147 x 4 mm Czech fire-polished beads Fuchsia (**B**)
- 147 x 4 mm cube beads Metallic Bronze Iris (**C**)
- 42 x size 11 seed beads Cranberry Gold Lustre (**D**)
-  2 x Czech pressed glass bell flower beads Milky Pink (**E**)
- Nylon beading thread pink
- Size 10 beading needle
- Conditioning wax
- Stop bead

The chart is read and worked from top-left start (x) to bottom right. Add more rows for a longer bracelet.

Row 1 Thread the needle with 2 wingspans of thread, condition lightly and add a stop bead to the end, leaving a 20-cm (8-in) tail. Using Square Stitch (see page 54), pick up 9 beads in the following sequence A B C A B C A B C and take down the thread to meet the stop bead **(fig. 2, row 1)**, This sets the first row of the chart for the cuff **(fig. 1)**.

Rows 2–48 Pick up an A in Row 2 and square stitch to the C of the previous row **(fig. 2, row 2.)** Continue working the chart until the cuff is 48 rows long (to fit a 15-cm/6-in wrist) or more for a longer bracelet. Add in new thread as required. Weave in the tail thread and trim.

ADDING THE CLASP BEADS (FIG. 3)
Rethread the needle with 1 wingspan of lightly conditioned thread.

Step 1 Pass up through the first 2 beads at the bottom of Row 7 of the cuff and out through the gap between the 2nd and 3rd beads (B and A). Pick up an E and a D and stitch back through the E, continue through the 3rd bead (A) and on through Row 7 until you come to the gap between the 7th and 8th beads (C and B).

Step 2 Pick up an E and a D and stitch back through the E,

continue through the beads of Row 7 to the top edge of the cuff. As you add each E and D, gently pull the thread so that the D is holding the E upright and flush with the cuff.

Step 3 Stitch back through the beads of Row 6 of the cuff and again through Row 7, securing the newly added beads. Continue following this thread path, coming back through Row 6 or 8 (either side of Row 7) until the bell flower beads feel secure. Weave the ends in and trim.

> **TIP**
> Remember to account for the clasp's overlap when estimating the length.

ADDING THE LOOPS (FIG. 4)

Rethread the needle with
1 wingspan of lightly
conditioned thread.

Step 1 Weave the thread through
the last few rows of the cuff
to anchor it, finally coming out
between the 2nd and 3rd bead
(B and A) of the last row. Pick up
20 D. Stitch back through the 1st
bead just picked up and continue
to stitch along the last row
coming out of the gap between

the 7th and 8th beads in the last
row of the cuff (C and A).

Step 2 Pick up 20 D. Stitch back
through the 1st bead picked up
and continue through the last
2 beads of the cuff. Stitch back
through the beads of Row 47.
Continue to follow this thread
path through the last 2 rows
of the cuff and the 2 loops
added until they feel secure.
Weave in the end and trim.

> **TIP**
>
> Do not force the needle
> through the size 11 (D)
> beads, as this can cause
> them to break.

STEP-BY-STEP DIAGRAMS

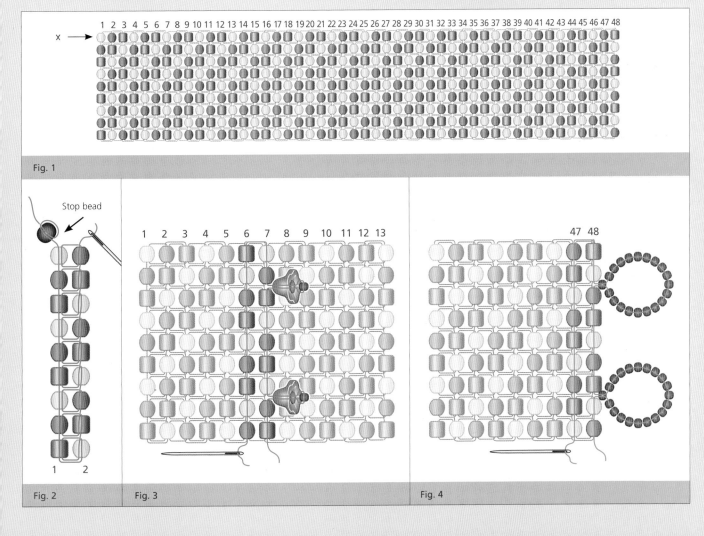

Fig. 1

Stop bead

1   2

Fig. 2

1 2 3 4 5 6 7 8 9 10 11 12 13

Fig. 3

47 48

Fig. 4

3 Brick Stitch

Like many beadweaving stitches, brick stitch has Native American origins, hence its alternative names of Cheyenne stitch or Comanche stitch. Brick stitch is named for the brick-like structure of the beadwork, though this simplification can be a little confusing as peyote stitch (see page 72) also shares this brick-like appearance.

Tools & Materials

- Size 8 seed beads
- Size 12 beading needle
- Beading thread
- Embroidery scissors
- Stop bead

A piece of brick stitch bends quite easily from side to side but with great reluctance from top to bottom, making a firm base for free-standing pieces, as well as for beading around focal beads or creating beaded shapes for charms, earrings and pendants. Combine it with peyote stitch, which is worked in a different direction, for more elaborate shapes.

Working in brick stitch requires a firm tension, but be careful not to work too tightly or the beadwork can buckle. Stop now and again to ease the beads flat on to the working surface to keep them in good order. Avoid working with a double thread, since this will present difficulties when you are trying to find the right thread to hook under.

FREEFORM BRACELET, *Lynn Davy*

Brick stitch is transformed in this cuff by using various-sized seed beads from size 11 to size 6 at random within an outline shape. This technique is known as freeform and doesn't have to be limited to brick stitch.

TYPES OF BRICK STITCH

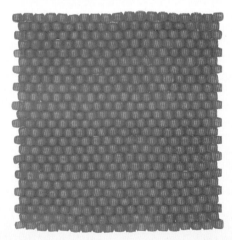

Brick stitch looks the same as peyote stitch (see page 72), but is worked from the bottom row upwards, rather than from side to side.

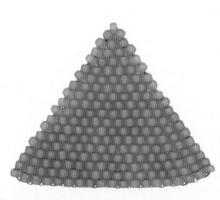

When shaping in brick stitch, take care to keep an even tension to avoid the edges distorting too much, especially over larger areas.

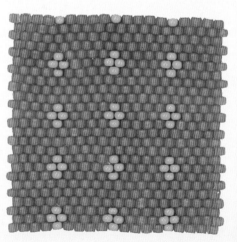

Beading colour patterns work well in brick stitch, as the design builds up row by row.

BRICK STITCH

The stitch is worked from a ladder-stitch base, illustrated here with turquoise beads for clarity.

Stop bead

STEP 1

Thread the stop bead and create a strip of beads using ladder stitch (see page 52).

STEP 2

With the thread coming out of the top of the last bead in the ladder, pick up 2 beads and pass the needle from the back of the work to the front, under the loop between the last and 2nd-to-last bead of the ladder strip.

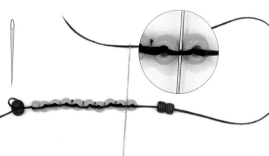

STEP 3

Pass the needle back up through the new left-hand bead and settle the beads so that the end sticks out from the strip below.

STEP 4

Pick up 1 bead and pass the needle under the next loop between the beads of the ladder below and back up through the bead just added.

STEP 5

Continue adding 1 bead at a time until you run out of loops to pick up. Finish with the thread coming out of the top of the last bead added. The brick wall is formed as you start each row with 2 beads, hooking the thread under the first loop of the previous row, and end each row by hooking the thread under the last loop of the previous row.

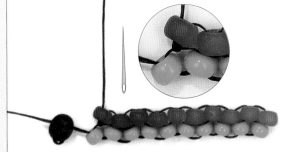

STEP 6

Start the next row by picking up 2 beads and passing the needle under the loop between the last 2 beads of the previous row and back up through the new right-hand bead just added.

DECREASING, INCREASING AND JOINS

Adding to or reducing the number of beads in a brick-stitch row allows quite intricate shapes to be worked. Add on larger areas of beadwork by incorporating ladder or peyote stitches into the work.

ONE-BEAD DECREASE

Start the row by picking up 2 beads and pass the needle under the 2nd loop, not the 1st as you have been doing. This draws the beads half-a-bead-width inward. If the 1st bead won't sit flat, thread round through the 4 beads again. Keeping the tension fairly relaxed will help avoid this.

Stop bead

Decreasing in this way at the beginning of every other row creates a diagonal line.

Decreasing in this way at the beginning of every row gives you a triangle/arrowhead.

FREEFORM BRACELET, *Lynn Davy*

Lynn softens brick stitch by using a mix of seed bead sizes and finishes. This creates a wavy, flowing texture that is all held together by the lovely analogous colour scheme and framed by the strong blue outline. Try going completely freeform using a bead soup (see page 39).

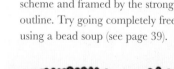

ONE-BEAD INCREASE: STEP 1

If you want to increase by more than half-a-bead-width, use ladder stitch to add on extra beads (shown in turquoise) at the beginning or the end of a row.

Stop bead

STEP 2

In the next row, brick stitch over the top of the ladder increase in the normal way.

STEP 3

Unlike a brick wall, you can build brick-stitch pieces from the bottom or the top, using the ladder strip as a central point. Weave the working thread down through the outer-edge beads until the thread comes out of the 1st bead in the ladder (don't draw too tightly or the sides will pull in). Turn the work.

STEP 4

Continue to work brick stitch as before.

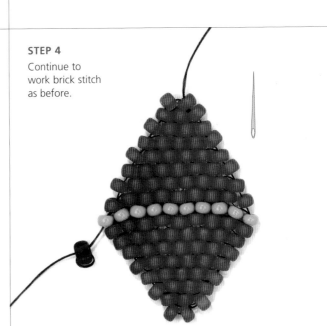

JOINS

The joy of brick and peyote stitches looking identical is that you can use the latter to add beads for a seamless join. The pictures at right show the beads being added vertically to a finished piece of brick stitch.

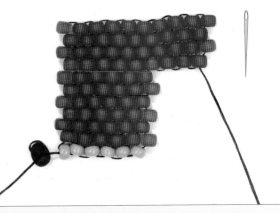

DESIGNER: MARY MARSHALL

Candy Heart Brooch

Clean, cheerful-coloured size 8 beads are used for this heart-warming brooch. Why not follow the same steps twice, using size 11 or cylinder beads to make two more hearts for a pair of coordinating earrings?

Tools & Materials

- 76 x matt lilac size 8 seed beads (**A**)
- 59 x matt pink size 8 seed beads (**B**)
- 3 x matt cream size 8 seed beads (**C**)
- Beading thread
- Size 10 needle
- Conditioning wax
- Stop bead
- Small bar pin brooch back

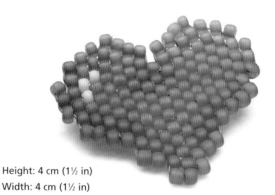

Height: 4 cm (1½ in)
Width: 4 cm (1½ in)

The chart is worked from the centre row, in 2 halves.

FIRST HALF OF BROOCH

Row 1 (centre row on chart)
Thread the needle with a wingspan of thread, condition lightly and add a stop bead to the centre of the thread, leaving the rest as a tail (for beading the 2nd half).
Start from the centre row of the chart and using Ladder Stitch (see page 52) bead 2A, 6B, 2A **(fig. 1a)**. Flip the row over so that the tail is emerging from the top of the 1st left-hand bead **(fig. 1b)**.

Row 2 Using Brick Stitch (see page 58), pick up 2A and pass the thread under the 2nd loop between the A and B on the previous row **(fig. 2a)**, stitch back through the 2A just added, through the 2A of the previous

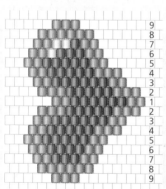

The heart shape is worked in 2 halves starting with the middle row, Row 1. Flip the beadwork when starting the second half and begin beading at Row 2. Use all B beads in rows 6 and 7 for the second half.

STEP-BY-STEP DIAGRAMS

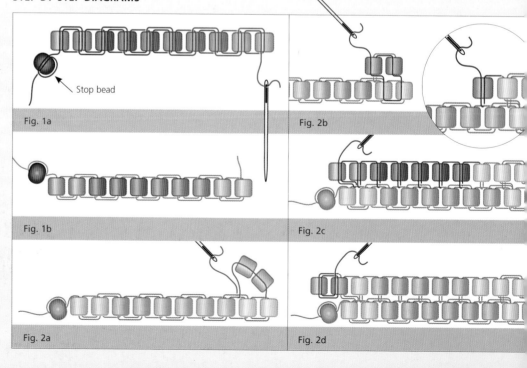

Fig. 1a — Stop bead
Fig. 1b
Fig. 2a
Fig. 2b
Fig. 2c
Fig. 2d

row and out again through the 2nd A **(fig. 2b)**.

Brick stitch along the row following the chart until the 10th bead. Pick up 1A and pass the thread through the same loop as for the 9th bead **(fig. 2c)**.

Pick up 1A and ladder stitch that to the 10th bead, passing the thread round twice to keep them in place **(fig. 2d)**.

Row 3 Step up by passing the thread through the loop between last 2 beads added **(fig. 3a)**. Using brick stitch, pick up 2A **(fig. 3b)**. Thread through these again **(fig. 3c)**. Finish Row 3 using brick stitch, following the chart.

Row 4 Pick up 2A and pass the thread under the 2nd loop along. Thread through once more to keep them in place **(fig. 4a)**. Continue in brick stitch along

Row 4, following the chart until the 9th bead. Pick up 1A and thread through the same loop as used for the previous A **(fig. 4b)**.

Row 5 Start as in Row 3, following the chart for Row 5.

Row 6 Start as in Row 4, following the chart for Row 6.

Row 7 Start as in Row 3, following the chart for Row 7.

Row 8 Start as in Row 4, following the chart for Row 8.

Row 9 Follow the thread path shown in fig. 5 so that your thread emerges from the top of the 2nd-to-last A bead in Row 8 **(fig. 5a)**. (If the beads are a little uneven, straighten them by going through the last 2 beads of that row again.)

Pick up 2A and pass the thread under the 2nd loop along. Brick stitch 1A **(fig. 5b)**.

Finish off the first half by threading back through the last row to straightening any misaligned beads, then back through the work to secure before trimming the end.

SECOND HALF OF BROOCH

Thread the needle with the tail thread. Stitch up and around through the 2A beads of Row 2 and back down to the 1st A of Row 1. Weave the thread back through this 1st row until the thread emerges from the penultimate A in the row **(fig. 6)**. Flip the work over so that the thread is now emerging from the top of the 2nd bead. Pick up 2A and pass the thread under the next loop (between the B and A of the row below) **(fig. 7)**.

Stitch back through the 2 beads to reinforce.

Continue with Row 2 to Row 9 for the 2nd half of the heart, remembering to omit the C beads.

ATTACH BROOCH BACK

Option 1 Using a separate length of thread (ideally Fireline) and an already bent needle, weave the thread through the beads and in and out of the brooch pinholes until firmly attached.

Option 2 Use a strong, clear-drying glue to stick the pin on. Option 1 is more time consuming but has the advantage of leaving the beadwork undamaged.

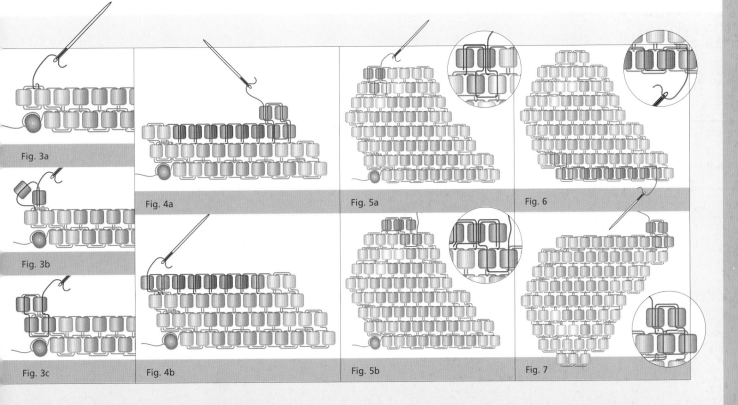

Fig. 3a

Fig. 3b

Fig. 3c

Fig. 4a

Fig. 4b

Fig. 5a

Fig. 5b

Fig. 6

Fig. 7

4 Herringbone Stitch

Herringbone stitch is also known as Ndebele stitch after the African people and region with which it was first associated. Like so many other historically regional stitches, the rest of the beading world has adopted and adapted it, making it one of the most useful techniques in a beader's toolbox.

Tools & Materials

- Size 8 seed beads in 3 colours
- Size 10 beading needle
- Beading thread
- Embroidery scissors
- Stop bead

The individual stacks of beads created by herringbone stitch work beautifully when combined with peyote stitch to make geometric shapes (see Beaded Shapes on page 110), and in its tubular form it is perfect for making supple, beaded ropes.

The stitch has two different starting methods; the ladder base is the easiest and the best place to start out. The baseless version is trickier to master, but gives the beader the advantage of being able to work from either end of the piece in hand, as well as giving a uniform finish.

Working herringbone in two colours highlights the beaded stacks as well as making it easier to follow the thread path. Keep the tension relaxed but not too loose; too tight and the work will bunch up. Finally, avoid the temptation to straighten out the beads – they are supposed to tilt towards each other in pairs.

FRILLY BUGLE COLLAR, *Jennifer Airs*

Bugle beads take on a lovely chevron form when used in herringbone stitch. The layers of netting stitch embellished with picot turns contrast well with these angular bugle beads. The collar is built up from a ladder-stitch base.

TYPES OF HERRINGBONE STITCH

Using 4 mm cube beads for baseless herringbone stitch shows off the stitch's stack structure, particularly at the ends.

Herringbone stitch with a ladder-stitch base worked in size 8 beads. You can see the slight tilt inward of each pair of beads.

Beading the swatch in two colours shows up the structure of the stitch as well as making it easier to follow when first learning the technique.

STEP 1

Thread the stop bead and create a strip of ladder stitch (see page 52), shown here in lime green, using an even number of beads. Make sure the thread is coming out of the top of the last bead in the ladder (bead 1).

Stop bead

STEP 2

Pick up 2 beads and pass the needle down through the next bead in the ladder (bead 2).

STEP 3

Pass the needle up through the next bead in the ladder (bead 3), pick up 2 beads and pass the needle down through the next bead in the ladder, ready to go through the next ladder bead along. Changing bead colour for each stack makes it easier to see the effect of the stitch.

STEP 4

Continue along the ladder, adding beads in pairs. At the end of the row, the thread will be coming out of the base of the ladder, but to add another row you need the thread to be coming out of the top of the ladder. To work the turn, pass the needle up through bead 9 of the ladder, then across and up through the last bead added in step 3. Now you are set for the next row.

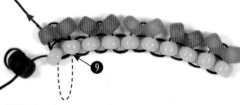

STEP 5

Continue back along the row, adding 2 beads at a time and working the turn at the end of each row. The stacks will sit slightly apart on even-numbered rows but will be linked together by working the next row.

DECREASING

Herringbone stitch does not lend itself to gentle decreasing, because changes have to be done two beads at a time.

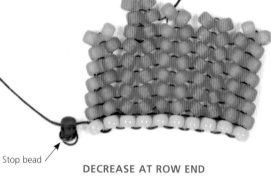

Stop bead

DECREASE AT ROW END

Just bead 1 stack fewer than the row below and work the turn for the next row up.

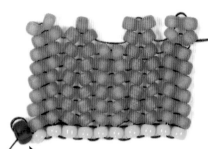

Stop bead

DECREASE MID-ROW

Work the row until you reach the stack where you want to insert the decrease. Skip over these 2 beads and pass the needle up through the 1st bead of the next stack. Work to the end of the row, as shown here. Tighten the thread to draw the work in before starting the next row and beading over the gap.

INCREASING

Shaping in herringbone stitch is usually done mid-row by gradually adding in new beads until another stack is created, or by working a few peyote stitches (see Beaded Shapes, page 110).

INCREASE AT ROW END

Using ladder stitch, extend the row below the increase by an even number of beads (shown in lime green). Then work in herringbone stitch along those beads and the rest of the row.

Stop bead

INCREASING MID-ROW
STEP 1

As you finish 1 stack, pick up a bead (shown in green) and pass up through the first bead of the next stack. The extra bead will sit on its side.

Stop bead

STEP 2

On the next row, pick up 2 beads over the extra bead from the previous row.

STEP 3

Repeat step 2. The 2 extra beads will start to sit like a new stack. By the third 2-bead increase, you will have an extra stack.

Stop bead

BASELESS TUBULAR HERRINGBONE

In this example, the new beads in each step are shown in green for clarity.

STEP 1

Pick up 6 beads and pass through them again to form a ring. Pass through the 1st bead again.

STEP 2

Pick up 2 beads and pass through the next 2 beads in the ring.

STEP 3

Pick up 2 beads and pass through the next 2 beads in the ring, making sure the thread does not twist.

STEP 4

Pick up 2 beads and pass through the last 2 beads in the ring and up through the 1st bead added in step 2; 3 beads in total. This is known as 'stepping up'.

STEP 5

The 3 stacks are now set in place. Pick up 2 beads, and pass down through the 2nd bead of the stack and up through the first bead of the next stack (shown here).

STEP 6

Repeat step 5 for the second stack.

STEP 7

Repeat step 5 and step up through the 1st bead of the pair added in that step. 3 stacks in total.

STEP 8

Tighten the thread so that the 3 stacks are drawn up into a short tube. Pick up 2 beads and pass down through the 2nd bead of the stack, then up through the 1st bead of the next stack.

STEP 9

Continue to add pairs of beads to each stack and step up at the end of each round by passing up through 2 beads of the 1st stack of the new round.

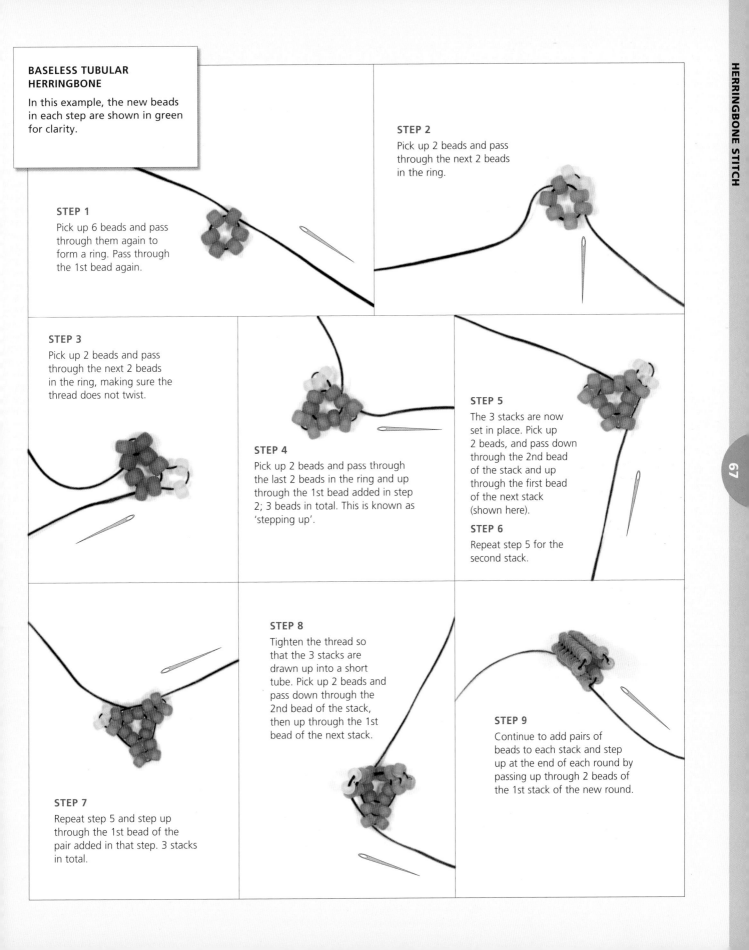

TUBULAR HERRINGBONE WITH LADDER BASE

In this example, the new beads in each step are shown in lime green for clarity.

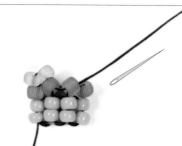

STEP 1

Make a ladder strip 6 beads long (or any even number) and 2 beads high. Join into a ring.

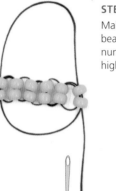

STEP 2

Pick up 2 beads and pass down through 1 of the next 2 beads in the ladder base and up through the next one. Add 2 more pairs of beads, stepping up through the 1st bead added at the end of the round, ready for the next round. Continue working herringbone around the tube.

STEP 3

Don't forget to step up at the end of each round or the rope will gradually spiral round instead of sitting straight.

CIRCULAR HERRINGBONE

By adding extra beads between the stacks of a tubular herringbone base, you get a circle. As the circle gets larger, the new beads form the base of new stacks. In this example, pink beads are used to illustrate the mid-row increases.

STEP 1

Work steps 1 to 4 for baseless tubular herringbone stitch (see page 67), finishing with a step up through the first stack.

STEP 2

Pick up 2 beads and pass down through the 2nd bead of the stack.

STEP 3

Pick up 2 beads and pass up through the 1st bead of the next stack

STEP 4

Repeat step 3 twice more and finish the round with a step up through the first stack.

STEP 5

Pick up 2 beads and pass down through the 2nd bead of the stack (as step 2). Pass the thread up through the 1st pink bead of the increase of the previous round. Pick up 2 beads and pass down through the 2nd pink bead and up through the 1st bead of the next stack. (You have made a new stack.)

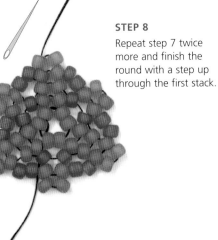

STEP 6

Repeat step 5 twice more and finish the round with a step up through the first stack. There are now 6 stacks in the circle.

STEP 7

Pick up 2 beads and pass down through the 2nd bead of the stack (as step 2). Pick up 2 beads and pass up through the 1st bead of the 1st new stack.

STEP 8

Repeat step 7 twice more and finish the round with a step up through the first stack.

STEP 9

Repeat steps 5 and 6, creating 12 new stacks altogether.

STEP 10

Pick up 2 beads and pass down through the 2nd bead of the stack and up through the 1st bead of the next stack.

STEP 11

Repeat step 11 around all 12 stacks, stepping up at the end of the round.

For a larger circle with more stacks, repeat steps 5–11.

DESIGNER: JANE LOCK

Friendship Bracelet

Friendship bracelets never go out of fashion. Traditionally designed with a tie fastening, these herringbone-stitched versions use a more conventional loop clasp. Quick and simple to bead, with unlimited colour options, you can make them sparkly, bright or colour coordinated. This is a great project for experimenting with different colour combinations.

Step 1 Thread a needle with 1½ wingspans of lightly conditioned braided monofilament beading thread. Make a ladder-stitch base using 4 A beads, leaving a 30-cm (12-in) tail for the clasp (**fig. 1**).

Step 2 Change to size 11 seed beads (B) and work 5 rows of herringbone stitch (see page 64) from the ladder-stitch base. (**fig. 2**).

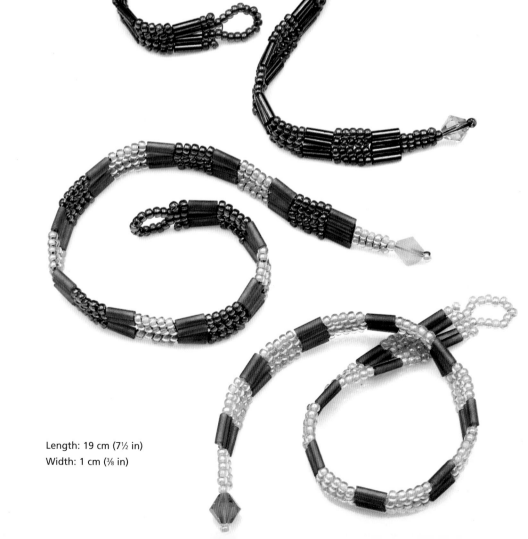

Length: 19 cm (7½ in)
Width: 1 cm (⅜ in)

Tools & Materials

36 x 6 mm bugle beads (No. 3) (**A**)

144 x size 11 seed beads (**B**)

1 x 6 mm bicone crystal (**C**)

- Braided monofilament beading thread
- Size 10 beading needle
- Microcrystalline wax

TIP
Use braided monofilament beading thread such as Fireline, since bugles have sharp edges that can cut through nylon threads.

Step 3 Work 1 row of herringbone stitch using 4 A beads. At this point the bugle beads should create a V-shape (**fig. 3**). Work 1 row of herringbone stitch using B beads; then a second row, which will pull the V together (**fig. 4**). Work 3 rows more using B beads. 5 rows in total.

Continue alternating 1 row of A beads with 5 rows of B beads until the bracelet is 1 cm (½ in)

shorter than the required length, finishing with a row of A beads (**fig. 5**).

ADDING THE LOOP

Step 4 Work 2 rows of herringbone stitch using B beads. Bring the needle out of the top of bead 2, pick up 2B and pass the needle back down through the top of bead 3, then up again through bead 2 and the 1st new bead added again (**fig. 6**).

Step 5 Pick up 12 B beads and pass the needle down through the 3 beads of the 3rd column, forming a loop. Pass the thread back up through the 2nd column and round the loop again. Repeat this thread path to reinforce the loop. Weave in the ends (**fig. 7**).

ADD THE TOGGLE

Step 6 Rethread the needle with the tail thread and position the needle so that it emerges from

the 2nd bugle bead. Using 2 B beads for each row, square stitch (see page 54) 5 rows (**fig. 8**).

Step 7 Pick up 1B, 1C and 1B. Thread back through C, B and then back down through the parallel column of beads. Reinforce the toggle by repeating the thread path until secure. Weave in the ends (**fig. 9**).

STEP-BY-STEP DIAGRAMS

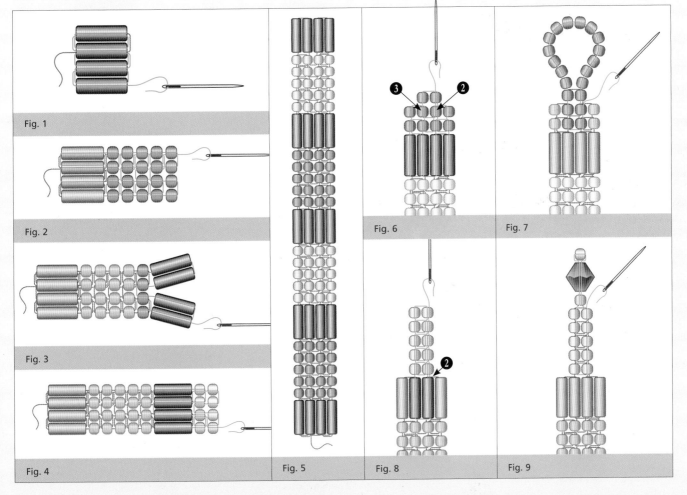

Fig. 1

Fig. 2

Fig. 3

Fig. 4

Fig. 5

Fig. 6

Fig. 7

Fig. 8

Fig. 9

5 Peyote Stitch

One of the oldest off-loom beadweaving stitches, peyote (or gourd) stitch is also one of the most versatile in the beader's lexicon.

Tools & Materials

- Size 8 seed beads
- Size 12 beading needle
- Beading thread
- Embroidery scissors
- Stop bead

In its simplest, flat form, peyote stitch can be used with an even or odd number of beads to make bands of beaded fabric; as tubular peyote stitch, it can be wrapped around stones, cabochons, even coins, to form a bezel or used as a beaded rope; circular peyote stitch is often combined with other stitches such as herringbone (Ndebele) or brick stitches as the backbone for 3-dimensional structures, shapes and textured designs.

Start with even-count peyote stitch and once mastered you will be ready to tackle all the variations: odd-count, two (or more)-drop, circular and tubular peyote stitches.

The first few rows of peyote stitch are always the hardest, getting the tension right and keeping the beads in place. The trick is to keep the tension firm, helping the beads to form their brick-like structure. I have used a stop bead here, but once you are familiar with the stitch you may find it easier to wrap the tail thread around the index finger of your non-working hand to counter the tension of the working thread.

CHERRY BLOSSOM NECKLACE, *Natasha VanPelt*

Open rings of circular peyote stitch using graduated sizes of seed beads are linked together by strung seed beads, larger beads and a beaded daisy chain to form a long and delicate necklace.

TYPES OF PEYOTE STITCH

Even-count peyote stitch is worked with an even number of beads in each row. Peyote-stitch rows are usually worked vertically, with beads from the previous row kindly sticking out to show you the way.

Odd-count peyote stitch is worked with an odd number of beads for each row, if your design needs a central point, like this diamond. As there is no bead to pass through at the end of every other row, it needs to be added in but following a figure-of-eight thread path (illustrated here for the 1st and continuing rows).

Peyote stitch can be worked using two, three or even four beads at a time to create different pattern effects. It can also speed up the beading if you are working a large area. Carol Dean Sharpe's project on page 150 uses three-drop peyote.

PEYOTE STITCH

In this example, the new beads in each step are shown in orange for clarity.

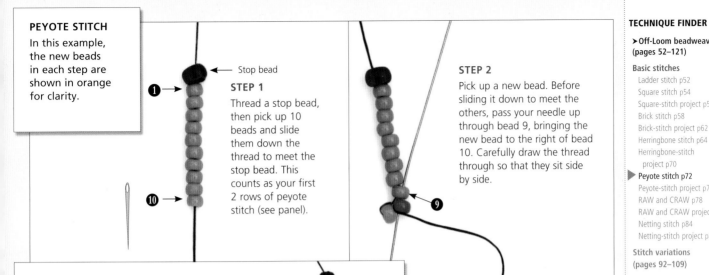

Stop bead

STEP 1

Thread a stop bead, then pick up 10 beads and slide them down the thread to meet the stop bead. This counts as your first 2 rows of peyote stitch (see panel).

STEP 2

Pick up a new bead. Before sliding it down to meet the others, pass your needle up through bead 9, bringing the new bead to the right of bead 10. Carefully draw the thread through so that they sit side by side.

Counting rows

There are two ways of counting rows in peyote stitch.
a) With the tail and working threads coming out at opposite corners, count the number of beads along the 2 edges and add them together (5+5=10).
b) Count the number of beads on the diagonal (10).

STEP 3

Keeping your working thread to the right, pick up a new bead. Pass your needle up through bead 7, bringing the new bead to the right of bead 8. Carefully draw the thread through so that they sit side by side.

STEP 4

Repeat steps 2 and 3 until your working thread is coming out of bead 1. You now have 3 rows of peyote stitch. Remember to try and keep the thread tight. This helps to keep the brick-like structure in place.

3 rows

STEP 5

Pick up a new bead and pass your needle down through bead 15, which is conveniently sticking out to show you the way.

STEP 6

Continue down the row, picking up a new bead and passing down through the bead sticking out from the previous row. Repeat these steps until you have the length required. If you prefer, you can flip the work at the end of each row so that you are always working in the same direction – but be careful to always keep the working thread and new beads to the right of your work.

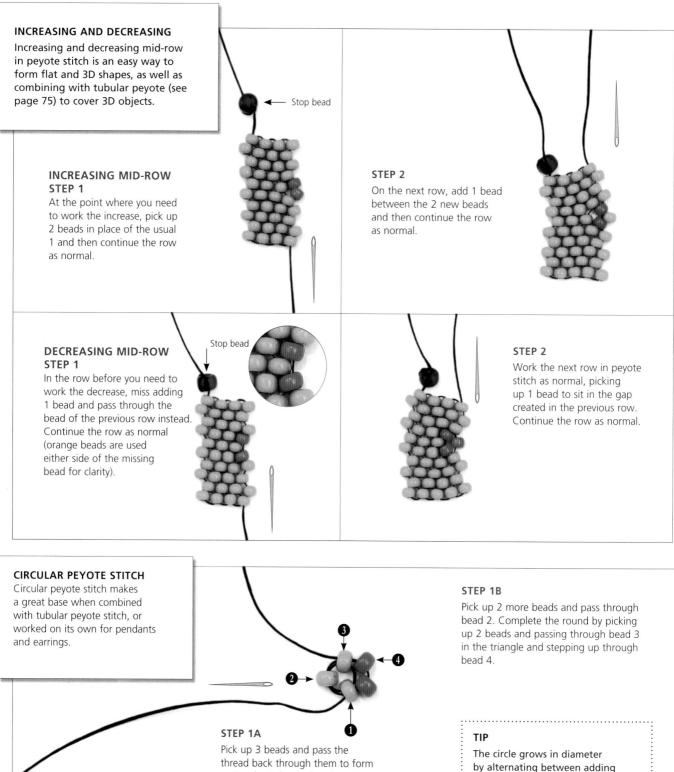

INCREASING AND DECREASING
Increasing and decreasing mid-row in peyote stitch is an easy way to form flat and 3D shapes, as well as combining with tubular peyote (see page 75) to cover 3D objects.

Stop bead

INCREASING MID-ROW STEP 1
At the point where you need to work the increase, pick up 2 beads in place of the usual 1 and then continue the row as normal.

STEP 2
On the next row, add 1 bead between the 2 new beads and then continue the row as normal.

Stop bead

DECREASING MID-ROW STEP 1
In the row before you need to work the decrease, miss adding 1 bead and pass through the bead of the previous row instead. Continue the row as normal (orange beads are used either side of the missing bead for clarity).

STEP 2
Work the next row in peyote stitch as normal, picking up 1 bead to sit in the gap created in the previous row. Continue the row as normal.

CIRCULAR PEYOTE STITCH
Circular peyote stitch makes a great base when combined with tubular peyote stitch, or worked on its own for pendants and earrings.

STEP 1B
Pick up 2 more beads and pass through bead 2. Complete the round by picking up 2 beads and passing through bead 3 in the triangle and stepping up through bead 4.

STEP 1A
Pick up 3 beads and pass the thread back through them to form a triangle. Pick up 2 beads and pass through bead 1 (shown here).

TIP
The circle grows in diameter by alternating between adding 2 beads at a time in the even-numbered rounds (step 1B onwards) and 1 bead at a time in the odd-numbered rounds.

74

TUBULAR PEYOTE STITCH

Tubular peyote stitch forms the basis of bezelling around a bead or stone (see Making Bezels, page 98) but can be used to make amulets, cover needle cases or cords or form 3D shapes. It is best worked around a knitting needle or a finger on your non-working hand for the first few rounds to ensure the beads form a tube.

STEP 1

Pick up an even number of beads and tie in a circle with 2 overhand knots. Pass the needle through the first couple of beads in the circle to hide the knot. Make sure the circle is not too tight.

STEP 2

Pick up a bead, and pass over a bead in the circle and through the next one, as if you were peyote stitching on the flat.

Last bead ← → 1st bead

STEP 3

At the end of the round, step up by passing through the last bead in the circle and the 1st bead added in this round. In this first round, take care not to let the circle twist, and always add beads to the right-hand side of the 'tube'.

STEP 4

Continue in peyote stitch, remembering to step up at the end of each round.

STEP 2

Pick up 1 bead and pass through the next bead from the previous round. Repeat this process until the round is complete (2 added beads shown here). Finish the round by passing through the last bead of the previous round and stepping up through the 1st bead added in this round.

STEP 3

Pick up 2 beads and pass through the next bead from the previous round. Complete the round by picking up 2 beads each time and passing through the next bead from the previous round. Step up at the end of the round by passing through the bead of the previous round and the 1st of the 2 beads added in this round.

STEP 4

Continue to grow the circle by repeating steps 2 and 3, remembering to step up at the end of each round.

DESIGNER: JANE LOCK

Leaf Motif Bracelet

A lovely combination of beadwork and sterling silver creates this fluid, sophisticated bracelet. Made from a variation on the classic peyote-stitch Russian leaf, each leaf is attached to the chain with a jump ring. You can vary the colours and size of the beads for different effects.

Tools & Materials

- 1960 x matt olive cylinder beads (**A**)

- 700 x matt grey cylinder beads (**B**)

- 385 x transparent green lustre cylinder beads (**C**)

- Beading thread in complementary colour
- Conditioning wax
- Size 12 beading needle
- 14 cm (5¾ in) sterling silver trace chain (8 links per inch)
- 36 sterling silver 4 mm (⅛ in) diameter jump rings
- 1 sterling silver 7 mm (¼ in) diameter jump ring
- 1 sterling silver clasp
- Chain-nose pliers

Using modified peyote stitch, make 35 leaf shapes (for a 16.5-cm/6½-in bracelet). The leaves are worked 1 side at a time:

Rows 1 & 2 Condition 45 cm (18 in) of thread and pick up 1B, 5A, 1C, 1A and centre them on the thread (you will use the other half of the thread for the second side of the leaf). Turn the work so that the 1B is at the top.

Row 3 Stitch up through the 4th-to-last bead to create a 3-bead picot at the bottom (**fig. 1**). Using A, peyote 2 stitches until your needle comes out of the top B.

Row 4 Using A, work 2 peyote stitches down towards the picot.

Row 5 Pick up 1C, 1A and work 1 peyote stitch up. Nudge the C so that it lies partially on its side. Pick up 1A and finish the row with a peyote stitch (**fig. 2**).

Row 6 Pick up 1A, 1B, 1A and stitch down through the first A, creating a 'T' shape with the B on the inside edge (**fig. 3**). Finish the row with 1 peyote stitch using A.

Repeat rows 5 and 6 until there are 4C beads on the outer edge (not including the picot). Work 1 more row 5 (**fig. 4**).

Flip the leaf over, rethread the needle with the long tail left in row 1 and work the second half in the same way, starting at row 4 (**fig. 5**). Once you have completed this, work the inner

edge. Stitch down through the B on the inside edge without adding any beads. Pick up 1B and stitch down through the next B.

Repeat until you have stitched through the centre B. Stitch down through an A to 1 side and back up through an A parallel to it and then up through the A to the left of the centre B, so that your needle is in the correct position to add the B beads on the other side (**fig. 6**).

Finally pick up 3B and close the leaf by stitching back down through the B beads on the opposite side of the leaf. Weave both ends in to secure and strengthen the leaf shape.

Using chain-nose pliers, join each leaf to the chain by linking jump

STEP-BY-STEP DIAGRAMS

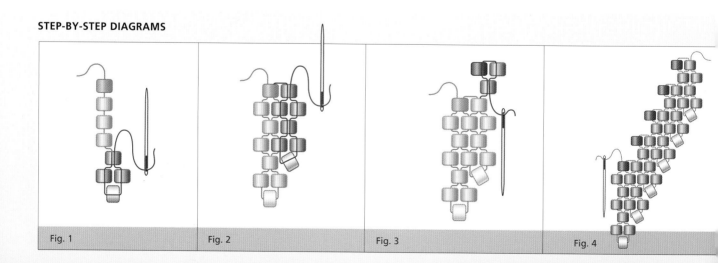

Fig. 1   Fig. 2   Fig. 3   Fig. 4

rings through them, then every
other chain link (**fig. 7**). Try to keep
each jump ring passing through the
links in the same direction.

Join a clasp to one end of the chain
with a 4 mm jump ring and add the
7 mm jump ring to the opposite
end, using the chain-nose pliers.

Length (including clasp):
18 cm (7 in)

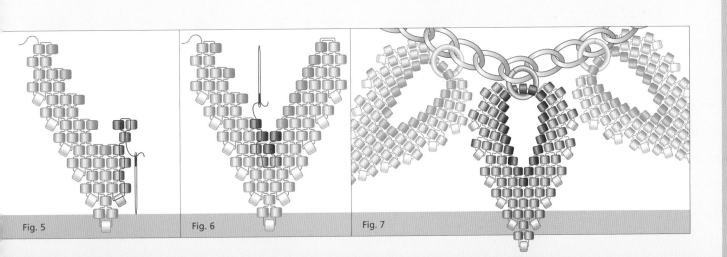

Fig. 5

Fig. 6

Fig. 7

6 RAW and CRAW

Right-angle weave stitch (RAW) was traditionally worked using two needles. Its renaissance in the beading world, together with its 3D cousin cubic right-angle weave (CRAW), owes much to the work of David Chatt and his exploration of the one-needle method that most beaders use today.

Tools & Materials

- Size 8 seed beads
- Size 10 beading needle
- Beading thread
- Embroidery scissors

Starting out in RAW and CRAW can be daunting at first, but the otherwise strange names provide a useful reminder of the thread path of the stitches; always turn a right angle before passing through the next bead. If the beads won't sit right, keep the following mantra in mind: top, side, bottom, side. This way, you are less likely to lose your place.

Maintaining an even tension is easier once you have a few rows stitched, especially if you pass the thread back through the beads to firm up the work for a good base on which to build.

Both RAW and CRAW are excellent stitches for embellishing, with corners that conveniently absorb extra beaded details.

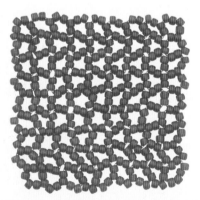

A ROSE IS A ROSE, *Julie Glasser*

Leaving CRAW unembellished highlights the architecture of the stitch, beautifully illustrated in this necklace. A monochrome colour palette of seed beads allows the eye to concentrate on the shapes, angles and texture of the necklace.

TYPES OF RAW AND CRAW

Keep repeating 'top, side, bottom, side' as you work in RAW. It will keep you focused on the thread path.

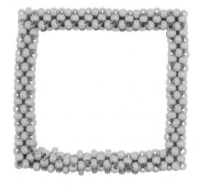

CRAW's versatility lies in the ability to build off any one of four sides of beadwork.

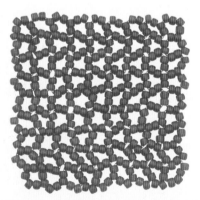

Using 2 beads for each top, side, bottom and side of a square makes it easier to work in RAW, but depending on your choice of beads the sides may not sit very straight.

RIGHT-ANGLE WEAVE (RAW)
In this example, the new beads in each step are shown in pink for clarity.

STEP 1
Pick up 4 beads and pass the thread through these 4 beads again, then the next bead, to form a cross shape.

STEP 2
Pick up 3 beads and create a second cross by passing back up through the right-hand bead that your thread is emerging from. Pass the thread through the 2nd and 3rd beads just added again. Remember that you turn a corner as you pass through each bead. You have now beaded 2 4-sided units with 1 side bead common to both.

STEP 3
Pick up 3 beads and repeat as for Step 2. This time the working thread will be emerging from the side bead in the opposite direction to the tail thread. Continue to build the first row of units, adding 3 beads each time and following the established figure-of-eight thread path.

STEP 4
When you reach the end of the first row of units, work your needle around each side of the last unit until it emerges from right to left through the bottom bead. This is easier to do if the thread is emerging downwards from the side bead. Now think of this as the top bead for the first unit of the 2nd row.

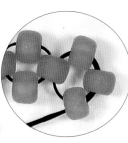

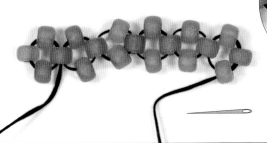

TIP
The steps here are photographed working left to right and back, but if it's easier you can flip the work at the end of each row so that you are always working in the same direction.

79

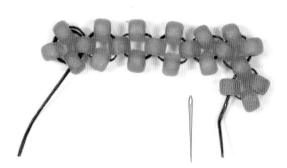

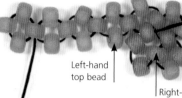

STEP 6
Pick up 2 beads. These will form the bottom and 1 side of the next unit. Pass the thread through the top bead, which is now shared with the unit above (pictured).

Left-hand top bead

Right-hand side bead

STEP 5
Pick up 3 beads and pass back through the top bead and down through the newly added side bead. You have now added the first unit of the second row.

STEP 7
Continue passing the thread down through the right-hand side bead. Go through the 2 new beads again and then the top bead of the next unit to the left.

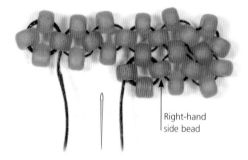

Right-hand side bead

STEP 9
Continue adding units along the Row 2 until you are ready to start the first unit of Row 3 with the thread emerging from the left-hand side of the last unit's bottom (bead 1). Pick up 3 beads for the side, bottom and side of the 1st unit and continue as before.

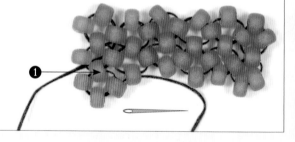

❶

STEP 8
Pick up 2 beads. Pass the thread up through the right-hand side bead, across through the top bead and down through the newly added left-hand side bead.

CUBIC RIGHT-ANGLE WEAVE (CRAW)
CRAW is a 3D stitch with 4 units of RAW forming the sides of a cube, and the top of the previous cube making the floor of a new cube.

STEP 2
Pick up 3 beads and create a second cross by passing back round through the right-hand bead your thread was emerging from in step 1 (bead 1). Without picking up a bead, pass the needle through the bottom bead of the first unit created in step 1 (bead 2).

❶

❷

STEP 1
Pick up 4 beads and pass the thread through these 4 beads again, then the next bead, to form a cross shape.

STEP 3

Pick up 2 beads and pass back through the bottom bead of the second unit (bead 1) and on through the bottom bead of the next unit (bead 2). Without picking up a bead, pass through the next bead (bead 3).

TIP

At this point, you may think you have broken the RAW 90-degree rule by beading in a straight line. But if you tilt the 2nd unit at right angles before threading on the 2 new beads, you will see that they are going to become the bottom and side beads of your first cube.

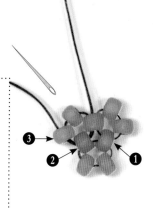

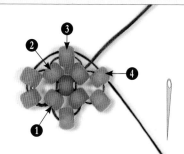

STEP 4

Pick up 2 beads and pass the thread back round through the side bead of the second unit (bead 1) and on back through the bead your thread has just emerged from (bead 2), the next bead round from that (bead 3) and then bead 4, as shown here.

At this point, fold the beadwork up to form the 1st cube unit minus a bottom bead, with beads 3 and 4 becoming the top and right-hand side beads.

STEP 5

Pick up 1 bead and pass up the left-hand side bead, completing the cube. Pass the thread through all four beads on this side of the cube again and on through the top and right-hand side bead. Tilt the cube 90 degrees towards you and pass the needle through the 4 beads facing you to secure the cube. Your thread is now emerging from the right-hand side of bead 1.

STEP 6

Pick up 3 beads and pass back through the bead your thread has just emerged from (this bead is hidden behind bead 3 in the picture) and on round through bead 2. These 3 beads should sit at right angles to the base unit, forming the first side of the next cube.

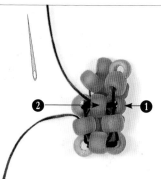

STEP 7

Pick up 2 beads and pass the needle through the bead marked 4 in the previous step, and on through bead 1 and bead 2.

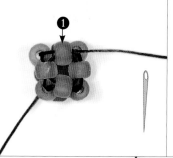

STEP 8

Pick up 2 beads and pass the needle down through the side bead (bead 1) and bottom bead (bead 2), shown here. Continue to pass on through bead 3.

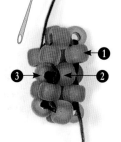

STEP 9

Pass up through the left-hand side bead (bead 1). Pick up 1 bead (bead 2) and pass the needle around all 4 beads of the side facing you and then around the 4 beads on the top of the cube to firm up the tension. Now the top of the cube is ready to provide the base for the next unit. Continue from step 6 to add more cubes.

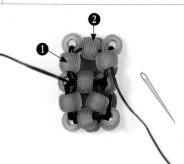

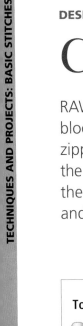

DESIGNER: JANE LOCK

Catherine Bangle

RAW is ideal for creating 3D pieces; each four-sided unit acts as a building block. The Catherine Bangle begins as a strip of flat RAW, which is then zipped up to form a tube. The same tube structure can be made using the CRAW method if you are comfortable with that technique. Embellishing the unit corners with 3 mm crystals and size 11 beads reinforces the tube and helps to create the curve of the bangle.

Tools & Materials

- 18 g size 8 Matt Lime Green AB seed beads (**A**)
- 76 x size 11 Sea Blue AB seed beads (**B**)
- 76 x 3 mm Rose bicone crystals (**C**)
- Braided monofilament beading thread
- Size 10 beading needle
- Microcrystalline wax

Inner circumference: 18 cm (7 in)
Outer circumference: 25 cm (10 in)

STEP-BY-STEP DIAGRAMS

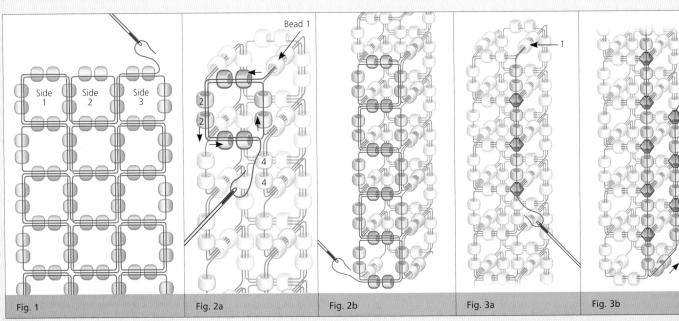

Fig. 1   Fig. 2a   Fig. 2b   Fig. 3a   Fig. 3b

Step 1 Thread the needle with 1½ wingspans of lightly conditioned thread. Picking up 2A each time, work a strip of RAW 3 units wide by 36 units long (**fig. 1**). You may need to add in extra thread (see page 43). Weave in the ends. Alternatively, create the strip using the CRAW method on pages 80–81 and skip straight to step 3.

Step 2 With a new length of conditioned thread, join the strip into a tube by creating the 4th side: position the thread so that it is coming out of bead 1 on side 3. Pick up 2A and pass the thread down through the 2 outer beads (marked 2) of side 1. Pick up 2A and pass the thread up through the 2 outer beads (marked 3) of side 3. Pass through 3 sides again, then down through the 2 side beads of the next unit down (marked 4) (**fig. 2a**). Continue to add the top/bottom of each unit, working your way in RAW down the strip (**fig. 2b**). Weave in the ends.

ADD EMBELLISHMENTS

Step 3 With a new length of conditioned thread, bring the needle out of bead 1 (**fig. 3a**). Pass down through the 2A of the next unit down. Pick up 1C, and following a straight line, pass the thread through the next pair of A beads. Continue adding 1C between side units for the length of the strip, stopping before the last corner. Turn the needle 90 degrees and pass through the bottom 2A to the 2nd side of the strip and up through 2A. Pick up 1C. Continue adding 1C to each corner until the last unit (**fig. 3b**).

Step 4 Pass the needle through the beads marked 1, 2 and 3 (**fig. 3c**). Pick up 1B and pass through the next 2A. Continue down this side and the last unembellished side as in step 3 (**fig. 3d**). NB. As the strip starts to curve on the 4th side, you may need to skip adding a B bead in some of the corners to keep the curve smooth. Leave

any thread loose for now to add in the final embellishments when the ends are joined.

JOIN THE BANGLE

Step 5 Bring the 2 ends together. The new A beads you add in this step 5 will form the sides of a new unit, with the top and bottom edges already provided by the ends you are joining together.

Add 2 pairs of A beads to form the first side of the new unit (**fig. 4a**). Bead round the unit again until the thread is emerging from the top of 1 side of the new unit. Turn the work slightly to pass the thread through the top beads of the next side round. Pick up 2A and pass through the sides of the unit until the thread emerges from the bottom of the 2 beads just added. Finish off the final side of this last unit following the established thread path (**fig. 4a**). Using the working and tail threads, work up and down the 4 sides adding in the missing C

and B beads (**fig. 4b**). Weave in the ends.

> **TIP**
> Using a new thread at the start of steps 2 and 3 makes it easier to undo any mistakes without the whole RAW strip unravelling.

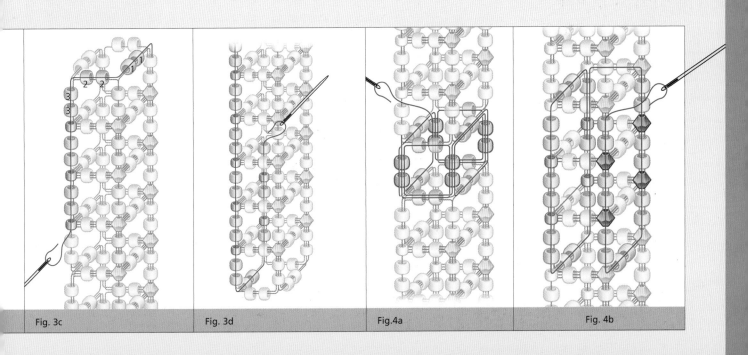

Fig. 3c   Fig. 3d   Fig.4a   Fig. 4b

7 Netting Stitch

Netted bead stitches are used across the world of beading – North America, Russia, Ukraine and Africa have all produced beautiful examples of traditional netted beadwork.

Tools & Materials

- Size 8 seed beads in at least 2 different colours
- A bead
- B bead
- Size 10 beading needle
- Beading thread
- Embroidery scissors
- Stop bead
- 5 mm (US size 8) double-pointed knitting needle for tubular netting (or similar-size straw)

Netted beadwork is fluid to the touch and has a beautiful drape, making it an ideal stitch for beaded embellishments on clothing or as covers; even baubles can be turned into an heirloom with a netted coat.

There are many types of netting stitch, but here we will concentrate on the simplest forms in order to understand and build on the technique: horizontal, vertical and circular netting. In appearance there is not a great deal of difference between vertical and horizontal netting; the difference lies in the construction and therefore the uses for the two versions. Circular netting opens up a further exciting dimension.

Netting is best worked with a relaxed tension and flat on the work surface, to begin with. You can always firm up the fabric by weaving the thread back through, or even using a double layer as in the Caribbean Cuff on page 88.

It is easier to use a contrast colour (B) for the 'cross' bead at least until you are familiar with the stitch.

FLOWER TILE, *Sarah Tucker*

Three earrings with the same pattern but different colour schemes give a very different effect. Here glass pearls and fire-polished beads act as the cross beads, with seed beads joining them together using a modified circular netting stitch.

TYPES OF NETTING STITCH

Basic circular netting stitch looks pretty when flat, but if this were a pop-up book you would see how it expands into a cone when held up from the centre.

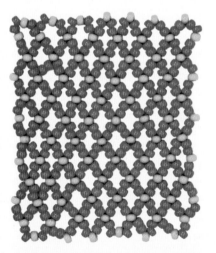

Vertical netting with five beads. Changing the number of beads between each cross bead alters the density of the beadwork. Count the cross bead and the number of beads either side of it to work out the number used.

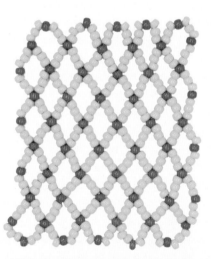

Vertical netting with seven beads creates a more open lattice in the beadwork.

VERTICAL NETTING
Vertical netting grows in length from left to right. The cross beads sit with the holes facing upwards.

STEP 1
Thread a stop bead and pick up 18 beads in following sequence: 1B, 2A, 1B, 2A, 1B, 2A, 1B, 2A, 1B, 2A, 1B, 2A.

Stop bead →

STEP 2
Turn to start the next row by passing the needle back through the 4th B bead (bead 4) from the needle.

STEP 3
Pick up 2A, 1B, 2A, skip the next B bead in the previous row, and pass the needle down through the last bead on the thread (B) before the stop bead.

STEP 4
Turn to start the next row by picking up 2A, 1B, 2A, 1B, 2A and passing the needle up through the B in middle of the loop from the previous row.

STEP 5
Pick up 2A, 1B, 2A, skip the next B bead in the previous row and pass up through the B in the middle of the top loop.

STEP 6
Turn to start the next row by picking up 2A, 1B, 2A, 1B, 2A and passing the needle down through the B in the middle of the loop from the previous row. Repeat steps 4–6 until the work is the right length.

85

NETTING CALCULATION
Unsure of how many beads to begin with? Decide whether you want 3-, 5- or 7- (call it X) bead netting and do the maths: (number of units in 1st row + 1) x (X +1). To make the turn, pass back through the bead, which is 2 x (X +1) back from your needle. At the turn end of each row, you will add half a unit so the netting is always one unit longer than the original length of the 1st row.

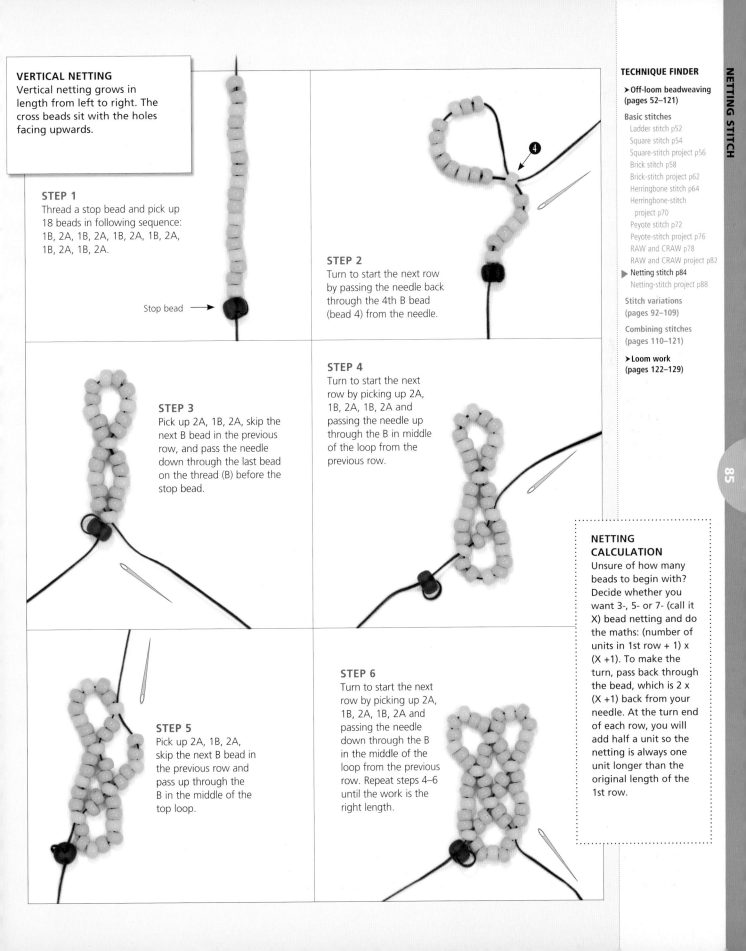

HORIZONTAL NETTING

Horizontal netting grows in length from top to bottom and is worked from a beaded base chain or fabric. The cross beads sit horizontally.

Create a length of beads either by stringing them on to cord or tigertail (with one end firmly anchored) or as has been used here, a strip of square stitch (see page 54). As before, it is easier to use 2 colours at first (A and B).

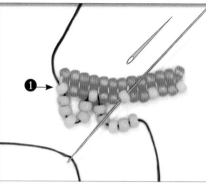

STEP 1

Exit the B bead (see bead 1) on the bottom row of the square-stitch strip, pick up 2A, 1B, 2A and pass the needle through the next B bead on the square-stitch strip. Continue to the end of the strip, looping 2A, 1B, 2A between the B beads.

STEP 2

Turn to start the next row by picking up 2A, 1B, 2A, 1B, 2A and passing the needle back through the 1st bottom B from the previous row.

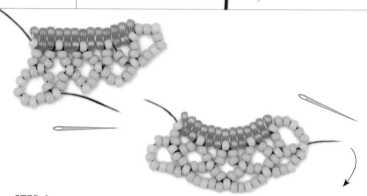

STEP 3

Pick up 2A, 1B, 2A and pass the needle through the B of the next loop. Continue with this step to the end of the row. At this stage, the beads will not sit correctly, but they will start to behave in subsequent rows.

STEP 4

Turn to start the next row by picking up 2A, 1B, 2A, 1B, 2A and passing the needle back through the 1st bottom B from the previous row (see above). Continue to the end of the row, as in step 3 (see above right). Repeat steps 2–4 for as long as required. You'll notice the curve in the square-stitch strip tends to increase with each row.

INCREASING AND DECREASING IN BOTH VARIATIONS

To increase, add an extra bead either side of the B bead in the loop you want to make larger (orange beads used here to illustrate).

To decrease, leave out a bead either side of the B bead in the loops you want to make smaller.

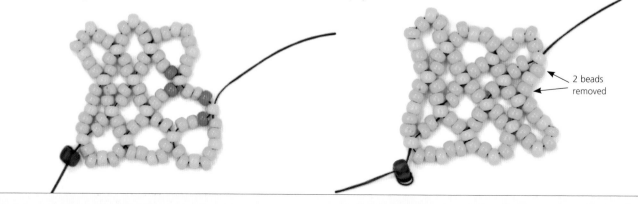

2 beads removed

CIRCULAR NETTING
Circular netting can be kept flat or used to cover curved surfaces.

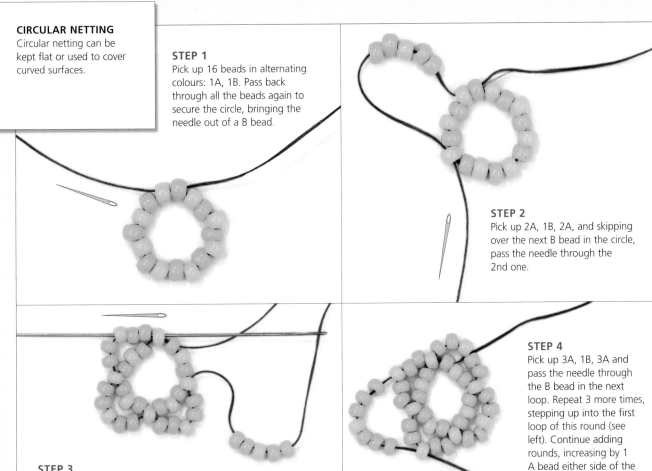

STEP 1
Pick up 16 beads in alternating colours: 1A, 1B. Pass back through all the beads again to secure the circle, bringing the needle out of a B bead.

STEP 2
Pick up 2A, 1B, 2A, and skipping over the next B bead in the circle, pass the needle through the 2nd one.

STEP 3
Repeat Step 2 twice more. On the 4th and final loop you need to 'step up' to the next round. Pass the needle through the B as usual, then instead of picking up new beads, pass the needle through the first 3 beads of the first loop added in step 2 so that the needle is coming out of that loop's B bead. Now you are ready to do the next round.

STEP 4
Pick up 3A, 1B, 3A and pass the needle through the B bead in the next loop. Repeat 3 more times, stepping up into the first loop of this round (see left). Continue adding rounds, increasing by 1 A bead either side of the B for each round until the circle is the required size.

TUBULAR NETTING
Tubular netting is worked in the same way as circular netting, but the number of beads in each loop remains the same instead of increasing each round. Pick up 12 beads 2A, 1B, 2A, 1B, 2A, 1B, 2A, 1B. Secure in a ring by passing the needle through the beads several times, coming out of a B bead. You will find this easier to do round a tube (near right, a 5 mm [US size 8] knitting needle has been used).

Continue to work in rounds with 2 A beads either side of a B bead.

DESIGNER: JANE LOCK

Caribbean Cuff

Netting stitches produce a lovely fluid fabric. Using a double layer of netting creates an almost elastic, self-supporting bangle that has the benefit of being reversible. It is worked here in size 8 beads to dramatic effect. Try using the same pattern with size 11 triangles, seed beads and 3 mm crystals for a more delicate bracelet cuff.

Tools & Materials

- 25 g size 8 seed beads Blue-lined Crystal AB (**A**)

- 5 g size 8 seed beads Matt Orange AB (**B**)

- 25 g size 8 seed beads Opaque Light Blue (**C**)

- 44 x 4 mm glass pearls Gold (**D**)

- Nylon beading thread gold
- Conditioning wax
- Size 10 beading needle

Inner circumference: 15 cm (6 in)
Outer circumference: 17.5 cm (6¾ in)

The cuff is worked in 2 layers, the first being the outer layer.

LAYER 1

Thread the needle with 2 wingspans of lightly conditioned thread and add a stop bead, leaving a 30-cm (12-in) tail. Try to keep your beading tension relaxed for this first layer.

Row 1 Pick up *1B, 2A, 1B, 2A* repeat from * to * twice until there are 22 beads.

Row 2 Pick up 2A,1D, 2A, 1B, 2A. Pass back through the 7th B bead counting from the tail end (**fig. 1a**). Pick up 2A, 1B, 2A, pass back through the 5th B from the tail on the 1st row. Repeat sequence twice, passing back through the 3rd and 1st B beads (**fig. 1b**).

Row 3 Pick up 2A, 1B, 2A, 1B, 2A. Pass back through the 4th B of row 2. Pick up 2A, 1B, 2A, pass back through the 3rd B of row 2. Repeat this sequence twice more,

passing back through the 2nd and 1st B (**fig. 2**).

Row 4 Pick up 2A, 1B, 2A, 1B, 2A. Pass back through the 5th B of row 3. Pick up 2A, 1B, 2A, pass back through the 4th B of row 3. Repeat this sequence twice more, passing back through the 3rd and 2nd B (**fig. 3**).

STEP-BY-STEP DIAGRAMS: LAYER 1

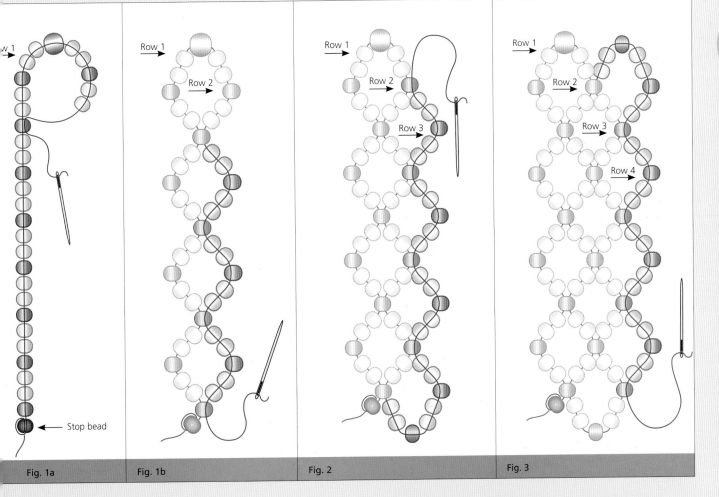

Fig. 1a   Fig. 1b   Fig. 2   Fig. 3

Row 5 Pick up 2A, 1D, 2A, 1B, 2A. Pass back through the 5th B of row 4. Pick up 2A, 1B, 2A, pass back through the 4th B of row 4. Repeat this sequence twice more, passing back through the 3rd and 2nd B (**fig. 4**).

Row 6 Pick up 2A, 1D, 2A, 1B, 2A. Pass back through the 4th B of row 5. Pick up 2A, 1B, 2A, pass back through the 3rd B of row 5. Repeat this sequence twice more, passing back through the 2nd and 1st B (**fig. 5**).

Repeat Rows 3–6 until the layer is almost long enough to go around your closed hand at its widest point (11 pearls on the top row,

10 on the bottom for this size). Repeat Row 3 once more. Do not weave the thread back through the layer. Depending on your tension for the 2nd layer, you may need to lengthen this layer before joining the 2 sides.

LAYER 2
Layer 2 is woven over the top of layer 1, C beads resting on A beads and sharing B beads, except at the long edges.

Rethread the needle with 2 wingspans of thread and work 2nd layer using C beads and a firmer tension, as follows:

Row 1 (worked over previous Row 3) Pick up 2C, 1 D, 2C and pass back through the 3rd B along the lower edge (**fig. 6**). Pick up 2C and stitch up through B of previous layer to the left. Pick up 2C and stitch up through the next B to the right. Continue up the previous Row 3, picking up 2C and stitching up through the Bs to the last cross (**fig. 7a**).

Row 2 Pick up 2C, 1D, 2C and pass back down through the 1st cross B to the right of the B from which the thread is exiting. Pick up 2C and pass back through the next B down and to the left. Repeat to the last cross B (**fig. 7b**).

Row 3 Pick up 2C, 1B, 2C and pass back up through the B to the right of the one just exited. Continue to pick up 2C beads and pass through the B beads, remembering to use a B over a layer 1 D and a D over a layer 1 B at each turn on the outer edges.

Stop 2 rows short of layer 1 (which you may need to lengthen if the cuff has shortened with the addition of layer 2) and join the layer 1 cuff edges together with the 2nd layer facing uppermost as follows:

STEP-BY-STEP DIAGRAMS: LAYER 2

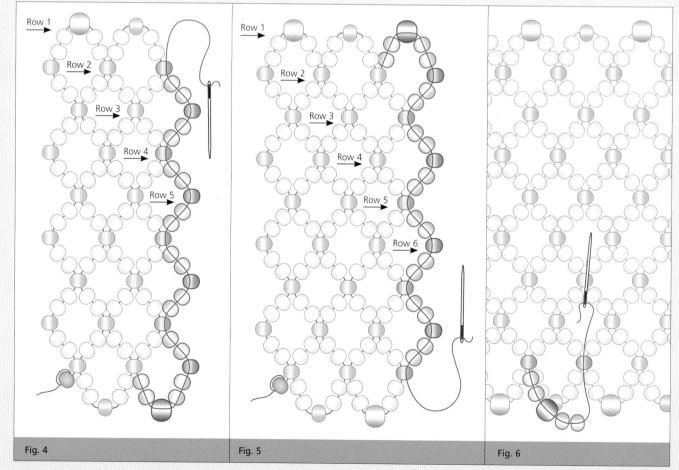

Fig. 4

Fig. 5

Fig. 6

Zip-up row (NB Depending on your finished length, the edges may have different B and D beads) With the thread coming out of the top B of the last row of layer 1, pick up 2A, 1B, 2A and pass back down through the 8th B added in the 1st row of layer 1.

Pick up 2A and pass back down through the next outer B of the last row of layer 1. Continue to pick up 2A and zigzag back and forth between the outer-edge Bs of the 1st layer until you reach the last B.

Pick up 2A, 1D, 2A and pass back up through the 1st B of Row 1 (**fig. 8**). Reinforce the join with the thread and trim.

Finish the 2nd layer following the pattern previously set and join the two ends. Turn the cuff so that layer 1 is uppermost. Weave the end back in and trim.

STEP-BY-STEP DIAGRAMS: LAYER 2 (CONT)

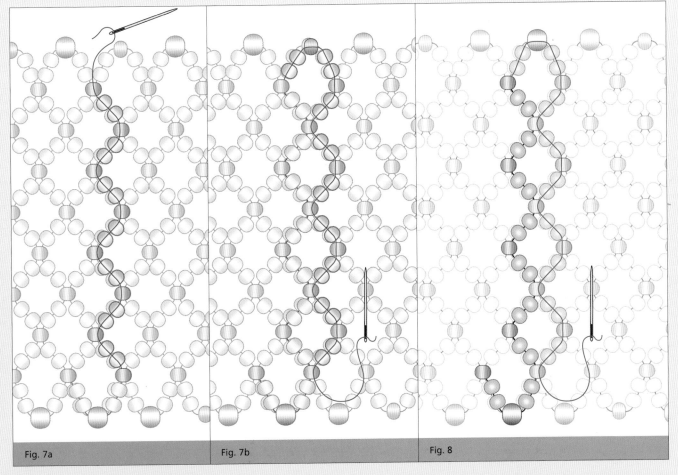

Fig. 7a　　　Fig. 7b　　　Fig. 8

8 Spiral Stitch

Spiral stitch is something of a generic name; there are many variations, spanning histories and continents. I've focused on spiral rope, my first and favourite beadweaving stitch, as well as a flat variation. Both are great places to start spiralling.

Tools & Materials

- Size 8 seed beads in at least 2 different colours
- Size 10 beading needle
- Beading thread
- Embroidery scissors
- Stop bead

LADY MADELEINE'S NECKLACE, *Helena Tang-Lim*

Supporting this stunning pendant is a sumptuous flat spiral-stitch rope of crystals and metallic gold seed beads. The pendant features a peyote-stitched bezel around a large Swarovski crystal. The bail at the top of the pendant is also made from bezelled crystals.

Spiral stitch's versatility comes from the huge variety of effects gained by simple changes in bead size and combination. Two colours of size 15 seed beads make a beautiful chain for elaborate pendants and beaded beads. Or mix size 11 and 8 beads with magatamas or semi-precious stones to make a glamorous bracelet. Flat spiral stitch is perfect for a bracelet or choker, dressed casually with matt seed beads and polished glass, or dressed up with pearls and Swarovski crystal.

Like many off-loom stitches, the first few steps are always the fussiest. Keeping a firm tension helps, as does starting off with a stop bead. Once you get to grips with the stitch, the spiral rope is best held in the hand, but working flat spiral stitch on the bead mat helps to keep the beads in the right place.

TYPES OF SPIRAL STITCH

Two-colour spiral stitch using size 8 seed beads shows off the core colour.

Flat spiral stitch using size 8 seed beads, along with 4 mm and 6 mm fire-polished beads.

Spiral stitch made with three colours and drop beads in the middle of each loop looks different to the two-colour sample.

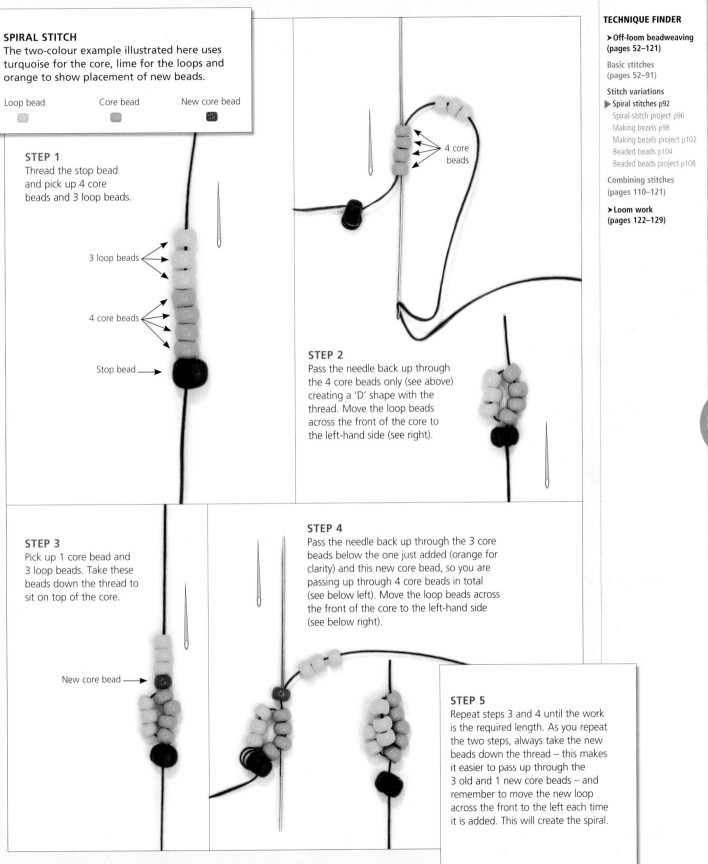

SPIRAL STITCH
The two-colour example illustrated here uses turquoise for the core, lime for the loops and orange to show placement of new beads.

Loop bead   Core bead   New core bead

STEP 1
Thread the stop bead and pick up 4 core beads and 3 loop beads.

3 loop beads →

4 core beads →

Stop bead →

STEP 2
Pass the needle back up through the 4 core beads only (see above) creating a 'D' shape with the thread. Move the loop beads across the front of the core to the left-hand side (see right).

4 core beads

STEP 3
Pick up 1 core bead and 3 loop beads. Take these beads down the thread to sit on top of the core.

New core bead →

STEP 4
Pass the needle back up through the 3 core beads below the one just added (orange for clarity) and this new core bead, so you are passing up through 4 core beads in total (see below left). Move the loop beads across the front of the core to the left-hand side (see below right).

STEP 5
Repeat steps 3 and 4 until the work is the required length. As you repeat the two steps, always take the new beads down the thread – this makes it easier to pass up through the 3 old and 1 new core beads – and remember to move the new loop across the front to the left each time it is added. This will create the spiral.

FLAT SPIRAL STITCH

Core beads work better if they are larger than the loop beads for this stitch. Here the core beads are orange size 6 beads and the loop beads are lime size 8 seed beads.

Tools & Materials

- Size 8 seed beads
- Size 6 seed beads
- Size 10 beading needle
- Beading thread
- Embroidery scissors
- Stop bead

STEP 1

Thread the stop bead and pick up 2 core beads and 3 loop beads.

3 loop beads

2 core beads

Stop bead

STEP 2

Pass needle back up through the 2 core beads, making a D-shape.

2 core beads

STEP 3

Move the loop beads across the front of the core to the left-hand side. Pick up 3 more loop beads and pass the needle up through 2 core beads as before.

The tension is loose in this picture to make it easier to see the thread path – make sure yours is tighter before moving on to step 4. Leave the second loop on the right-hand side of the core (below).

3 loop beads

STEP 4

Pick up 1 core bead and 3 loop beads. Pass the needle back up through the top 2 core beads (1 from the previous step, 1 just added). Move the loop across the front to the left-hand side.

Core bead

STEP 5

Pick up 3 loop beads. Pass the needle up through the 2 top core beads. Leave this loop on the right-hand side of the core.

STEP 6

Repeat steps 4 and 5 until the work is the required length. Remember that in step 4 the loop moves to the left and in Step 5 it stays on the right. You need to make sure that the new loop always sits on top of the previous loop.

Flat spiral stitch bead variation

Flat spiral stitch is more effective with beads of varying sizes and finishes. Combine 6 mm and 4 mm crystals, pearls or fire-polished glass with size 8 or size 11 seed beads (use 4 beads either side of the 4 mm bead). Here the core beads are 6 mm fire-polished glass beads, and the loops size 8 seed beads (A) and 4 mm glass beads (B). Note that 4 mm beads sit in the gap between the 2 core beads (see step 4).

STEP 1
Thread the stop bead and pick up 2 core beads then 3 loop beads A, 1 loop bead B and 3 loop beads A. 7 loop beads in total.

STEP 2
Pass the needle back up through the 2 core beads, making a D-shape (as in step 2, opposite).

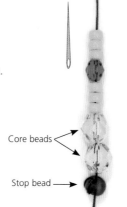

Core beads

Stop bead

STEP 3
Move the loop beads across the front of the core to the left-hand side. Pick up 7 loop beads in the colour formation as for step 1, and pass the needle up through the 2 core beads as before. Leave this loop on the right-hand side of the core.

STEP 4
Pick up 1 core bead and 7 loop beads in the colour formation as before. Note that the core beads should sit on top of each other, with the B loop beads sitting either side of the top core bead. Pass the needle back up through the top 2 core beads (1 from the previous step, 1 just added).

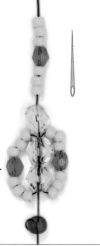

B loop beads are in line with gap between 2 core beads

STEP 5
Continue working in flat spiral stitch, adding 7 beads for each loop until the work is the required length.

95

VARIATIONS
Spiral stitches can look totally different with just a subtle change to bead finishes and sizes.

Small beads make a good 'chain' for pendants. Size 11 beads in 2 colours are used here.

Varying bead sizes and introducing new colours within the same spiral can make a feature of the spiral effect. Here size 8 beads have been used for the core and middle bead in each loop and size 11 beads have been used for the rest of the loop.

Use magatamas or drop beads in the centre of the loop for extra texture.

DESIGNER: JANE LOCK

Spiral Necklace

Tools & Materials

⬤ 10 g size 11 seed beads Gold Lined Crystal **AB** (**A**, loop)

⬤ 10 g size 11 seed beads Matt Bronze (**B**, core)

⬤ 1 x 90-cm (36-in) strand peridot tumble chips (**C**, loop)

- Nylon beading thread gold
- Conditioning wax
- Size 12 beading needle
- Toggle clasp

Spiral stitch's versatility lies in the mix of beads that can be used in the technique. Uniform seed beads create a perfect rope-like length, but add a few magatamas or crystals and you have a completely different look. In the Spiral Necklace, we've used size 11 gold-hued seed beads and peridot tumble chips, but the pattern works just as well with size 8 beads and larger tumble chips or even pearls or crystals.

Length (including clasp): 46 cm (18 in)

The necklace is beaded as 1 rope and divided into 3 sections using different-sized C beads. Each section is approximately 14 cm (5½ in) long.

To create the graduated effect, sort the tumble chips into 3 piles of tiny, small and medium/large chips. Discard any with broken holes.

You will need to add in new thread a few times, but tumble chips are quite sharp so keep the lengths to no more than 1½ wingspans or it will start to fray.

Step 1 Thread the needle with 1½ wingspans of conditioned thread, pick up 4B, 3A and stitch a Spiral (see Spiral Stitch, page 93). Bead 4 more spirals using 1B, 3A each time. 3 beads in the loop (**fig. 1**).

Step 2 Pick up 1B, 1A, 1 tiny C, 1A and spiral stitch as before. 3 beads in the loop. Continue using the tiny Cs for approximately 7 cm (2¾ in), (**fig. 2**).

Step 3 Pick up 1B, 1A, 1 small C, 1A and spiral stitch as before. 3 beads in the loop. Continue using the small Cs for approximately 7 cm (2¾ in.), (**fig. 3**).

Step 4 Pick up 1B, 1A, 1 small C, 1 medium C, 1 small C, 1A and spiral stitch as before. 5 beads in the loop. Continue using 5 beads in the loop for approximately 14 cm (5½ in). If you want a really chunky centre section, start adding in some more medium and large Cs in the middle of the necklace for about 2 cm (¾ in)

when the overall length is approximately 21 cm (8¼ in), (**fig. 4**).

Finish the necklace by repeating Steps 1–3 in reverse order, so that you finish with Step 1.

TIP
As you reach the centre, it will become harder to bead through the 4 core (B) beads at once so don't try. Go through 1 or 2 at a time, keeping the thread from twisting as you do so. Your needle will begin to look a little mangled. Don't worry – this is normal.

ADDING THE TOGGLE CLASP

Using the tail thread with a size 12 needle attached, stitch through the bottom ring of half of the toggle clasp. Stitch back down through 8 core beads and back round up through the 5th loop, 4 core beads and toggle clasp (**fig. 5a**). Repeat, reducing the number of core beads by 1 and coming back up through the 4th, 3rd and 2nd loop and corresponding core beads each time (**fig. 5b**). It will get quite difficult to pass the needle through the beads so take care not to break any. Once you are happy the clasp is secure, take the thread back down through the core towards the centre and trim. Repeat for the other half of the clasp.

STEP-BY-STEP DIAGRAMS

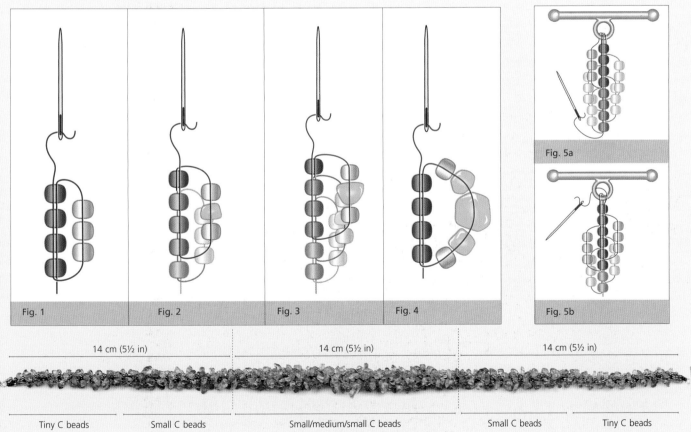

Fig. 1   Fig. 2   Fig. 3   Fig. 4   Fig. 5a   Fig. 5b

14 cm (5½ in)   14 cm (5½ in)   14 cm (5½ in)

Tiny C beads   Small C beads   Small/medium/small C beads   Small C beads   Tiny C beads

9 Making Bezels

Beaded bezels are a perfect way to incorporate larger, flat stones or beads with pointed backs, such as cabochons and rivolis, into your beadwork. Rivolis, being uniform in shape and size, are the best place to start. Of course, it helps that they are sparkly, small and available in a huge range of glorious colours, bringing out the magpie in all of us.

Tools & Materials

- Size 8 seed beads
- Size 11 seed beads
- Size 15 seed beads
- 12 mm diameter crystal rivoli
- Size 12 beading needle
- Braided monofilament beading thread
- Craft scissors

Traditionally, 0.1 mm or 0.12 mm braided thread and cylinder beads, together with size 15 and tiny size 15 Czech charlottes, are used for bezelling around a rivoli of any size, but the steps shown here are worked with size 8, 11 and 15 seed beads around a 12 mm rivoli. Not much of the rivoli is left showing, but it is a good way to practise the technique.

The principle of working in tubular peyote or RAW stitch, with beads of decreasing sizes to create a little cup, is the same whatever the shape of the bead or cabochon, but RAW bezels are easier to fit around an awkward shape.

PEACOCK DREAMS, *Lynn Davy*

The centrepiece of this necklace is the luminous labradorite cabochon in a RAW bezel. The chain is made by combining tubular peyote stitch and circular RAW, joined by links of flat RAW with a few subtle embellishments. Using the restrained metallic colour palette adds to the drama of the piece.

TYPES OF BEZEL

18 mm rivoli bezelled with the tubular peyote-stitch method, using size 11 cylinder beads, size 15 beads and size 15 Czech charlottes.

Changing the colours of beads used in the bezel can change the appearance of the rivoli. Here the size 15s and charlottes are reflected in the rivoli's surface.

18 mm rivoli bezelled with RAW and tubular peyote stitch, using size 11 seed beads, size 11 cylinder beads and size 15 seed beads.

PEYOTE STITCH BEZEL
Braided monofilament is a good thread to use on bezels, as the tension needs to be tight and crystals can have sharp edges.

STEP 2
Using tubular peyote stitch (see page 75), work 1 round of size 8 beads, stepping up through beads 1 and 2 at the end of the round. Working around a knitting needle or finger stops the ring of beads from twisting.

STEP 1
Using a half wingspan of conditioned braided monofilament, pick up 20 size 8 seed beads and tie into a ring using a square knot. Pass through the 1st 2 beads again so that the knot is hidden.

STEP 3A
Change to size 11 seed beads and continue in tubular peyote stitch for a further 2 rounds, stepping up at the end of each one.

STEP 3B
In adding the 2nd round of size 11 beads, they won't sit properly until you remove the knitting needle and allow the cup shape to form.

STEP 4
Add 1 last round of size 15 seed beads to reinforce the cup.

The differing bead sizes have now created a cup shape ready to take the bezel.

TIP
Previous beaders have worked out the number of cylinder beads needed to fit around a rivoli so you don't have to:

Rivoli diameter	Number of size 11 cylinder beads in 1st ring
12 mm	30
14 mm	36
16 mm	40
18 mm	46

STEP 5

Pass the needle back through the bezel to the other side of the work, following a diagonal thread path.

Front with size 15 seed beads   Back

STEP 6

Drop the rivoli into the cup with right side down and repeat steps 2, 3 and 4 (if necessary) to secure it in place. Weave in the ends.

RAW STITCH BEZEL

To work out the length of RAW needed, wrap the RAW strip around the circumference of the cabochon or rivoli until it is approximately one unit shorter than required.

STEP 2

The new beads in this step are shown in turquoise for clarity. Join the strip into a ring by picking up 1 side bead, passing through the top bead from 1 end of the strip, picking up 1 side bead and passing through the bottom bead from the opposite end of the strip. Pass the thread through this last unit again to reinforce it (shown here), finishing with the working thread emerging from the side bead of the next unit (bead 1).

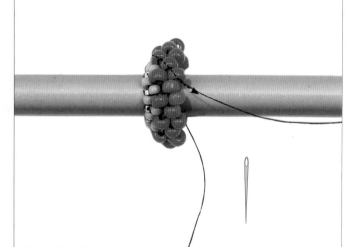

STEP 1

Using a half wingspan of braided monofilament and size 8 seed beads, weave a strip of RAW (see page 79) 9 units long, to fit a 12 mm rivoli.

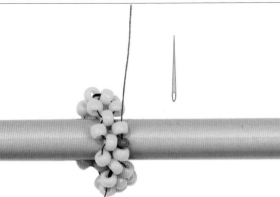

STEP 4

Step up by passing through the first size 11 bead added. Still using size 11 seed beads, work the next round in tubular peyote stitch, stepping up through 2 beads at the end of the round.

STEP 3

Using size 11 seed beads, pick up a bead and pass the needle through the next side bead. Continue to add a bead between each side bead of the RAW units all the way around the ring.

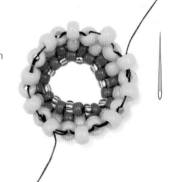

STEP 5

Work a final round of tubular peyote stitch using size 15 seed beads to reinforce the cup.

STEP 6

Pass the needle back through the bezel to the other side of the work, following the established thread path.

STEP 7

Drop the rivoli into the cup with right side down and repeat steps 2 and 3 to secure it in place. Weave in the ends.

Front with size 15 seed beads

Back

TIP

I find bezelling with RAW works best using rocailles (round seed beads), not cylinder beads.

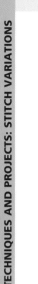

DESIGNER: JANE LOCK

Santa Fe Pendant

Sometimes it is best to let sparkly things speak for themselves, and a rivoli can be pretty sparkly. This pendant enhances the basic peyote-bezelled shape with an embellishment of beads around the edge, a hanging loop and a beaded 'chain'. You can use a metal chain if you prefer, but I rather like the slightly rock-chick effect of the square-stitched chain.

A size 13 needle is very fine and it will get bent out of shape. Don't worry: use the curve to help get around some of the trickier corners. Use braided monofilament beading thread for the bezel, but it is better to use a nylon thread for the cord to keep the beadwork supple.

Tools & Materials

▮ 5 g size 11 Matt Olive Gold cylinder beads (**A**)

▮ 1 g size 15 Gold Lustred Cranberry seed beads (**B**)

- 14 mm crystal rivoli
- Braided monofilament beading thread
- Nylon thread for the cord
- Size 13 beading needle
- Size 12 beading needle
- Lobster clasp
- Split ring

Cord length: 43.5 cm (17 in)
Pendant: 2 x 2 cm (¾ x ¾ in)

TIP
Refer to page 73 for instructions on how to count rows in peyote stitch.

Step 1 Thread the size 13 needle with 1 wingspan of conditioned braided monofilament beading thread and make a bezel around the rivoli using the technique described on page 99, in the following sequence: bead 1 row of peyote stitch using A and 2 rows of peyote stitch using B (**fig. 1**).

Step 2 Weave the thread through the beadwork to the outer edge of the bezel and on to the centre row of cylinder beads. Bring the needle and thread out of a raised bead.

Pick up A and pass the thread through the next raised A bead. Continue to add a total of 15 A beads in this manner (**fig. 2**), leaving a gap for adding the tab in the next step. You have just 'stitched in the ditch'.

MAKE A TAB

Step 3 Pick up 1 B and peyote stitch into the next ditch. Repeat once. Using these 2 beads as a foundation, continue to peyote stitch a strip until it is 22 rows long. Fold the strip in half so that the last edge meets the first 2 B beads. The raised beads of both ends will fit together like the teeth of a zip (**fig. 3**). If not, add 2 more B beads in peyote stitch to the working end of the tab. Then pass the thread through these 4 beads to 'zip' them up. NB. Do not worry if this bends your needle out of shape; use the bend to get at the awkwardly placed beads at the top of the bezel.

MAKE THE CORD

Step 4 Thread a size 12 beading needle with a 1½ wingspan of nylon thread and, using the A beads, make a cord approximately 40 cm (16 in) in length, using the 2-bead square stitch method on page 55 (**fig. 4**).

TIP
When making the cord I prefer not to condition the thread for this technique, as the beadwork can get clogged with wax.

Step 5 Slip the pendant over the cord and add a clasp and split ring at each end by retracing the thread path for as many times as the bead holes will take and then securing the ends (**fig. 5**).

STEP-BY-STEP DIAGRAMS

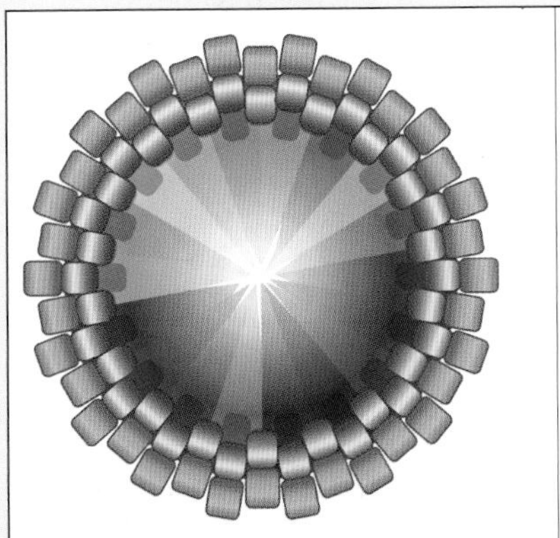

Fig. 1

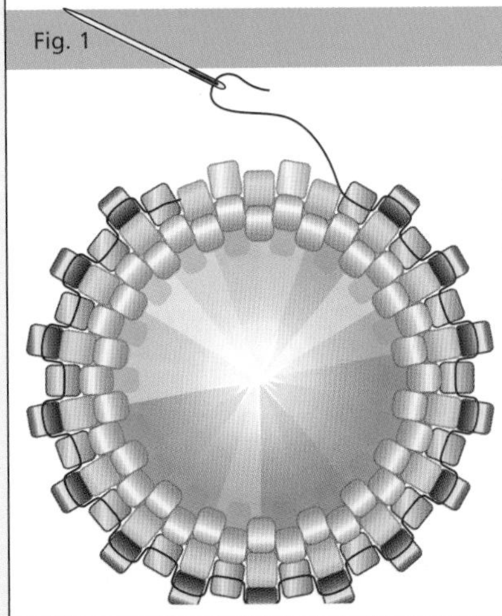

Fig. 2

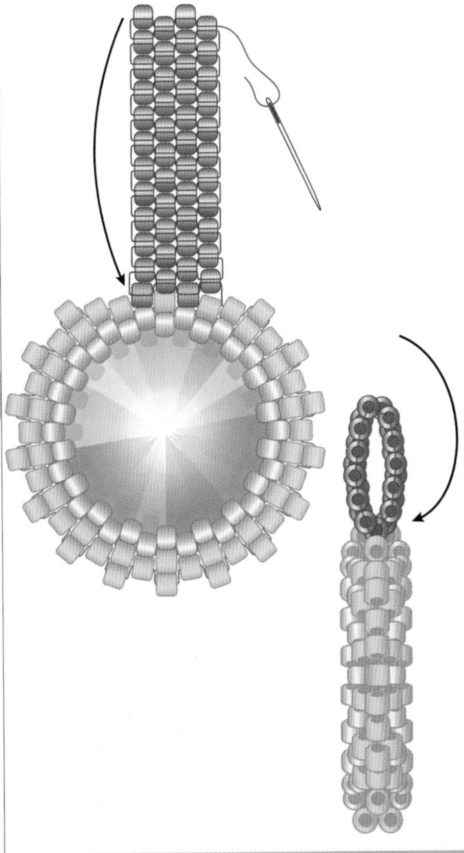

Fig. 3

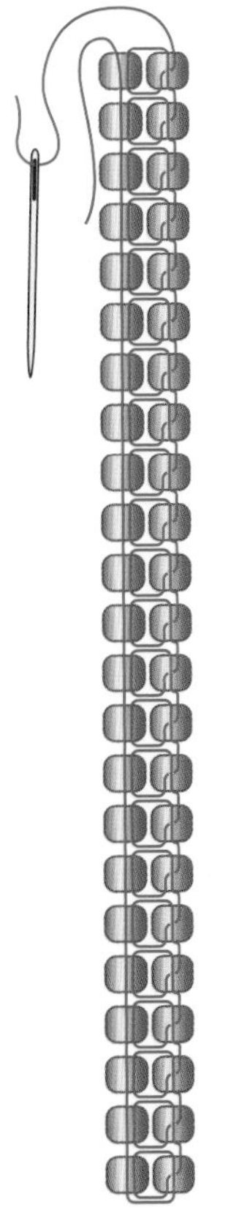

Fig. 4

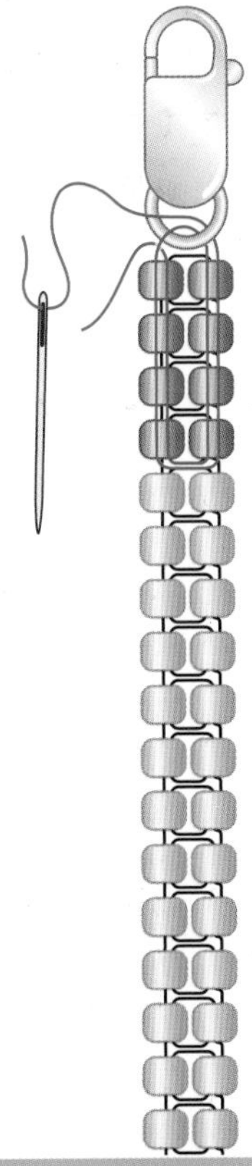

Fig. 5

10 Beaded Beads

Not content with the millions of beads already available to them, beaders have gone on to find ways of making their own.

Tools & Materials

- Size 8 seed beads (**A**)
- 6 mm glass pearls (**B**)
- Size 11 seed beads (**C**)
- 4 mm glass pearls (**D**)
- Embroidery scissors
- Beading thread
- Size 10 beading needle

GALAXIES BEAD BEADS,
Jennifer Airs

Modified netting stitch can make fabulous beaded beads. The cluster effect of these beaded beads, made with bicone crystals in those glowing AB colours, contrasts beautifully with the smooth, deep shine of the unique lampwork focal beads.

Those with a scientific bent have, in recent years, explored the similarities between molecule structures and beaded beads – there is even an entire blog dedicated to the topic (see Resources on page 156). Some beadweavers have taken the mathematical approach to coming up with new bead combinations to make increasingly complex, beautiful spheres and other shapes.

For those of you firmly taken outside their comfort zone by this approach (and I include myself in this group), we have designed a beautiful self-supporting beaded bead that can be used to make bold jewellery (see The Beaded Bead Necklace on page 108). This technique uses modified netting stitch, but some beaded beads use a wooden bead as their base and are then covered over with shaped peyote stitch.

TYPES OF BEADED BEADS

Small beaded bead made using a mixture of 6 mm bicone crystals and glass pearls.

Medium beaded bead (size as shown in the demonstration) made using a mixture of 6 mm bicone crystals and glass pearls.

Large beaded bead made a mixture of 6 mm bicone crystals and glass pearls (see diagram over the page).

FIRST HALF OF THE BEAD

The bead is worked in two halves. Position the beads for step 1 in the centre of the thread, leaving a long tail with which to work the second half of the bead.

STEP 1

Thread a needle with a ¾ wingspan of stretched thread and pick up 10 beads in the following order: 1A, 1B, 1A, 1B, 1A, 1B, 1A, 1B, 1A, 1B. Centre the beads on the thread and then tie in a ring.

STEP 2A

Pass the needle through the next A once more. Pick up 3C, 1A, 3C and pass through the next A. Repeat a further 4 times until the round is complete.

Step up

STEP 2B

Step up by passing through the 1st 3C added and the next A.

STEP 3

Pick up 1D and pass through the next A added in step 2. Repeat a further 4 times until the round is complete. 5 D beads in total. Up to this point, you can work clockwise or anticlockwise. From step 4 onwards, work around the ring in an anticlockwise direction.

STEP 4

Tighten the thread to pull the D beads inwards and upwards so that they sit on top of the C beads to start the curve of the bead.

STEP 5

Pick up 2C, 1A, 2C and pass through the next A, added in step 2. Push these beads in towards the centre (don't worry if they don't stay there just yet). Keep the tension tight for the next steps.

— Step 2A

New A

STEP 6

Pick up 1C and pass back up through the 3rd C added in step 5. Tighten the thread away from this bead. This will form a little triangle of C beads with the thread emerging from the top C (this can be seen clearly in step 11 over the page).

A from step 2

3rd C

STEP 7

Pick up 1A, 2C and pass through the next A from step 2.

STEP 8

Pick up 1C and pass back up through the 1st C added in step 7, thus forming a second triangle of C beads.

STEP 9

Repeat step 7.

STEP 10

Repeat step 8, making a third triangle of C beads.

STEP 11

Repeat step 7.

Triangle of beads

STEP 12

Repeat step 8 to make the 4th triangle of C beads, each with 1A bead to its left (marked 1, 2, 3, 4, far right).

1st C added in step 7

STEP 13

Pick up 1A, pass down through the 2nd C added in step 5, pick up 1C and pass through the next A to complete the 5th triangle of C beads and the round.

2nd C added in step 5

New C added in step 13

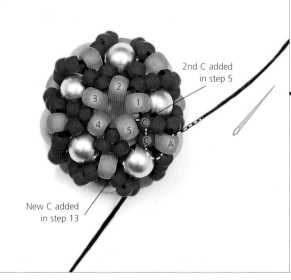

STEP 14

Pass back through the next D and A, then up through the C beads to the top centre ring of 5 A and D beads. Thread through this ring a few times to reinforce the shape, then weave the end in, trim and turn over.

SECOND HALF OF THE BEAD

Rethread the needle with the tail thread (now your working thread) and continue as for the first half of the bead from step 2 to step 13.

BEADED BEAD VARIATIONS

By working more or fewer rounds and changing the number of beads in each round, you can create larger or smaller beaded beads. The following steps and diagrams illustrate one variation to the basic technique with reference to the photographs on the previous pages. Like the medium beaded bead, this step-by-step variation is worked in two identical halves.

Tools & Materials

- 48 x size 8 seed beads (**A**)

- 6 x 6 mm crystal bicones (**B**)

- 204 x size 11 seed beads (**C**)

- 12 x 6 mm crystal-coated pearls (**D**)

- 12 x 4 mm crystal bicones (**E**)

LARGE BEADED BEAD

In the diagrams the bead is beaded in a clockwise direction. You can go round either way, but it is important to be consistent within each beaded bead.

Round 1 Follow the instructions in step 1 (see page 105) but pick up 24 beads in the following order: 1A, 1C, 1B, 1C, 1A, 1C, 1B, 1C, 1A, 1C, 1B, 1C, 1A, 1C, 1B, 1C, 1A, 1C, 1B, 1C, 1A, 1C, 1B, 1C (**fig. 1**).

Round 2 Using A and C beads, follow the instructions in step 2 (see page 105) for a total of 6 times (**fig. 2**).

Round 3 Using D beads, follow the instructions in step 3 (see page 105) for a total of 6 times (**fig. 3**).

Round 4 Repeat Round 2 (**fig. 4**).

Round 5 Using E beads, repeat Round 3 (**fig. 5**).

Round 6 Follow the instructions in step 4 (see page 105) (**fig. 6**).

Round 7 Follow the instructions for steps 5–14 (see pages 105–106), ending with a total of 6 A beads (**fig. 7–11**). Return to the tail thread to bead the second half, starting with Round 2.

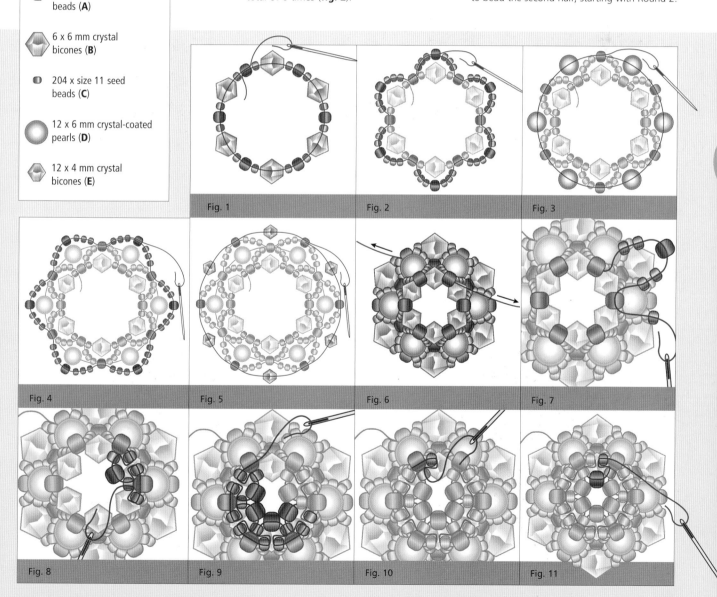

Fig. 1

Fig. 2

Fig. 3

Fig. 4

Fig. 5

Fig. 6

Fig. 7

Fig. 8

Fig. 9

Fig. 10

Fig. 11

DESIGNER: JANE LOCK

Beaded Bead Necklace

I struggled with a name for this dramatic piece, but finally settled on the obvious. The necklace uses the medium-sized beaded bead technique on pages 105–106. You can add or reduce the number of beads to adjust the length, but always use an odd number so that there is a beaded bead at the centre of the necklace.

Tools & Materials

- 7 medium beaded beads (see page 104) each using:

  - 25 x silver size 8 seed beads (**A**)

  - 5 x 6 mm aquamarine fire-polished Czech glass beads (**B**)

  - 90 x dark matt pink size 11 seed beads (**C**)

  - 10 x 4 mm aquamarine fire-polished Czech glass beads (**D**)

For the necklace:

- 8 x 6 mm silver fire-polished Czech glass beads
- 8 x 4 mm aquamarine fire-polished Czech glass beads
- 8 x 4 mm fuchsia fire-polished Czech glass beads
- 3 x 60-cm (24-in) lengths 0.3 mm tigertail
- Magnetic clasp
- 2 x calottes
- 4 x crimps
- Chain-nose pliers
- Round-nose pliers
- 2 x jump rings
- Side cutters

Step 1 String 1 beaded bead on to the centre of all 3 strands of tigertail (**fig. 1**).

Step 2 String 1 x 6 mm silver bead on to 1 strand of tigertail, 1 x 4 mm aquamarine bead on to the 2nd strand and 1 x 4 mm pink bead on to the 3rd strand (**fig. 2**).

Step 3 String another beaded bead on to all 3 strands of tigertail. Continue adding beads in this sequence, first to one side and then the other, until all 7 beaded beads are strung with groups of 3 beads in between. Finish either side with a group of 3 beads (**fig. 3**).

Step 4 Attach the clasp, one side at a time: string all 3 strands through a calotte, making sure the hook end faces away from the beads (**fig. 4 inset**). String 2 crimps on to all 3 strands (**fig. 4**).

Step 5 Position the crimps approximately 13 cm (5 in) or more for a longer necklace from the last beads and close firmly using the chain-nose pliers (**fig. 5 inset**). Trim the tigertail with the side cutters to within 1 mm (1/32 in) of the crimps.

Step 6 Bring the calotte up to meet the squashed crimps and fold it over so that the crimps

are hidden inside. Pinch each 'hinge' closed with the tip of the chain-nose pliers – this will firmly close the calotte around the crimps. Using the round-nose pliers, turn the hook at the end of the calotte into a closed loop (**fig. 6**).

Step 7 Using the chain-nose pliers, open 1 of the jump rings. Use the open jump ring to join half the clasp to the loop of the calotte. Close the jump ring with a reverse-twist action, keeping the ends as close together as possible (**fig. 7**).

Repeat steps 4–7 for the second half of the clasp.

STEP-BY-STEP DIAGRAMS

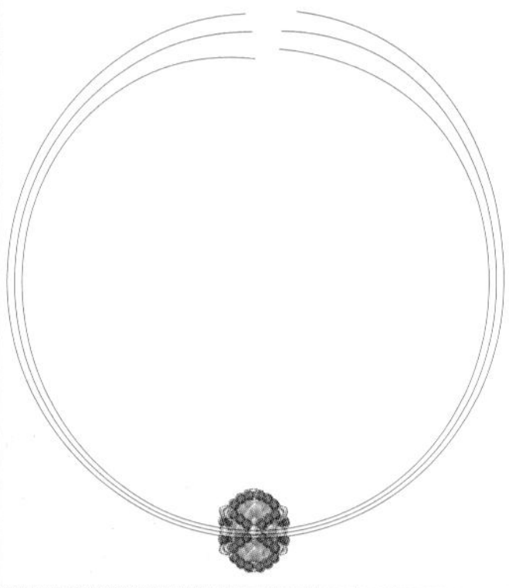

Fig. 1

Fig. 2

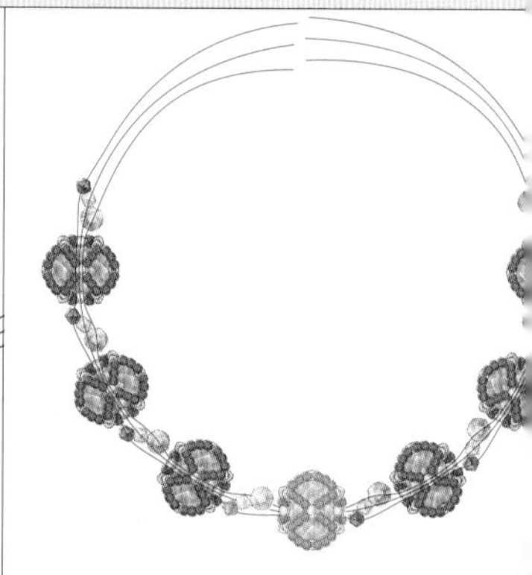

Fig. 3

Tigertail length: 47 cm (18½ in)
Beads: 1.5 cm (⅝ in)

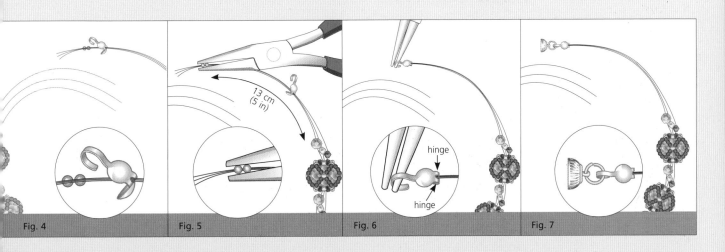

Fig. 4

Fig. 5

13 cm
(5 in)

Fig. 6

hinge

hinge

Fig. 7

11 Beaded Shapes

Tools & Materials

- Size 8 seed beads
- Size 10 beading needle
- Beading thread
- Embroidery scissors

We have already seen how certain beadweaving techniques can be combined to build beadwork (ladder stitch as a base for brick and herringbone stitches) or to create bezels. When it comes to making geometric shapes, the combination of peyote stitch and herringbone is hard to beat.

A triangle made with three stacks of herringbone and increasingly wide peyote sides is just the starting point. Cylinder beads are most often used in this type of geometric work, because their straight sides click together so satisfyingly, but they can seem tiny at first. Starting out with size 8 seed beads as in this example is less daunting, yet no less satisfying. It does help to use the best-quality Japanese seed beads you can find, however, as the uniformity of each bead helps to build into a better shape.

ALL TOGGLED UP, *Julie Glasser*

Hexagon-shaped rings and strips of peyote stitch zipped up into tubes make great toggle clasps. Here the designer has taken the idea a step further and joined each toggle with another flat strip of peyote stitch to make the ultimate adjustable necklace.

TYPES OF BEADED STITCH

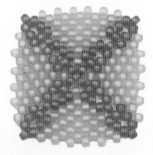

Square using size 8 seed beads in two colours.

Square using size 11 cylinder beads in two colours.

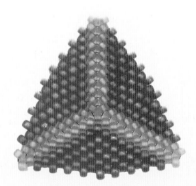

Triangle using size 8 seed beads in two colours.

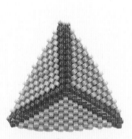

Triangle using size 11 cylinder beads in two colours.

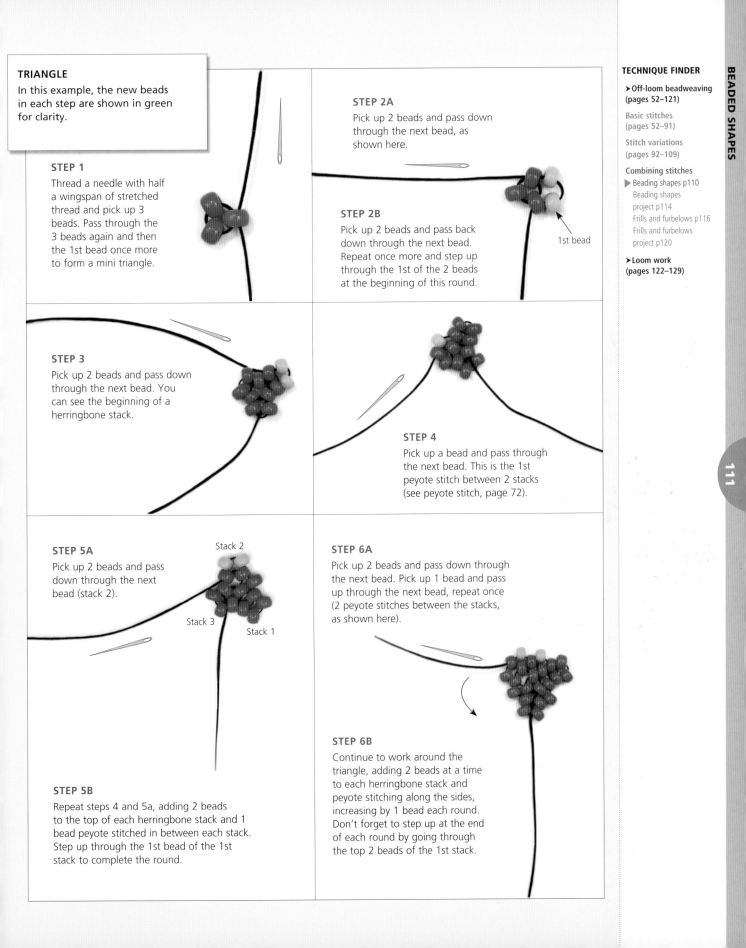

TRIANGLE

In this example, the new beads in each step are shown in green for clarity.

STEP 1

Thread a needle with half a wingspan of stretched thread and pick up 3 beads. Pass through the 3 beads again and then the 1st bead once more to form a mini triangle.

STEP 2A

Pick up 2 beads and pass down through the next bead, as shown here.

STEP 2B

Pick up 2 beads and pass back down through the next bead. Repeat once more and step up through the 1st of the 2 beads at the beginning of this round.

1st bead

STEP 3

Pick up 2 beads and pass down through the next bead. You can see the beginning of a herringbone stack.

STEP 4

Pick up a bead and pass through the next bead. This is the 1st peyote stitch between 2 stacks (see peyote stitch, page 72).

STEP 5A

Pick up 2 beads and pass down through the next bead (stack 2).

Stack 2

Stack 3

Stack 1

STEP 5B

Repeat steps 4 and 5a, adding 2 beads to the top of each herringbone stack and 1 bead peyote stitched in between each stack. Step up through the 1st bead of the 1st stack to complete the round.

STEP 6A

Pick up 2 beads and pass down through the next bead. Pick up 1 bead and pass up through the next bead, repeat once (2 peyote stitches between the stacks, as shown here).

STEP 6B

Continue to work around the triangle, adding 2 beads at a time to each herringbone stack and peyote stitching along the sides, increasing by 1 bead each round. Don't forget to step up at the end of each round by going through the top 2 beads of the 1st stack.

SQUARE

The square is built slightly differently, with rounds alternating between peyote stitch and herringbone stitch. This is noted in the steps to help you keep track. In this example, the new beads in each step are shown in green for clarity.

STEP 1

Thread a needle with half a wingspan of stretched thread and pick up 4 beads. Pass through the 4 beads again and then the 1st bead once more to form a cross.

STEP 2

Pick up 1 bead and pass back down through the next bead. Pick up 1 bead and pass down through the next bead. Do this twice more until there are 4 new beads in the round. Step up through bead (see bead 1).

STEP 3: PEYOTE STITCH WITH PEYOTE INCREASE IN THE CORNER

Pick up 3 beads, skip a bead and pass through the next corner bead (as shown here). Do the same for the remaining 3 sides. Each group of 3 beads is the corner of the square. Keep the tension loose at this stage; although the centre of the 3 beads will stick out (X), you need to push it into a straight line for the next round. Step up through bead (see bead 1).

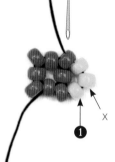

STEP 4A: PEYOTE WITH HERRINGBONE IN THE CORNER

Pick up 2 beads, skip the middle bead of the 3 added in the last round (X) and pass down through the next bead. This is where you need to push that demanding X bead back into place. Pick up a bead and pass up through the next bead. This single bead is effectively peyote stitch.

STEP 4B

Repeat around the remaining sides of the square. End the round by stepping up through the bead (see bead 1).

STEP 5: PEYOTE WITH HERRINGBONE IN THE CORNER

Pick up 2 beads and pass down through the next bead. Pick up a bead and pass through the next bead. Pick up a bead and pass through the next bead (2 peyote stitches), as shown here. Repeat around the remaining sides and step up through bead (see bead 1).

STEP 6: PEYOTE STITCH

Peyote stitch 1 bead at a time around all 4 sides, then step up through bead (see bead 1).

TIP

When you step up at the end of the round, you are passing through 2 beads at a time: the last bead in the step you are working and the 1st bead added at the start of the current round.

STEP 7: PEYOTE STITCH WITH PEYOTE DECREASE IN THE CORNER

Peyote stitch 1 bead at a time along the 1st side. Pass through the corner bead without adding any beads. Repeat along the remaining sides and step up so your working thread emerges from the bead (see bead 1).

STEP 8: PEYOTE WITH PEYOTE INCREASE IN THE CORNER

This round is similar to step 3. Start by working 3 peyote stitches along the side. Pick up 3 beads, skip the corner bead and pass down through the next bead, as shown here (remember that bead X will have to be poked down into place in the next round). Repeat around the remaining sides, stepping up through bead 1 at the end. Note that with each round, you step up 1 bead further along the side.

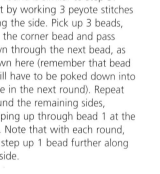

STEP 9: PEYOTE WITH HERRINGBONE IN THE CORNER

Peyote stitch 3 beads along the side and add 2 beads in herringbone to the corner, pushing the middle bead into its position as the corner bead. Continue around the remaining sides and step up through bead (see bead 1).

STEP 10

Repeat step 9.

STEP 11

Repeat step 6.
You can continue to grow the square by repeating steps 7 to 11. Remember to keep the tension loose on the corners of step 8 to keep the square flat.

DESIGNER: JANE LOCK

Pyramid Earrings

Layering shaped beadwork creates an interesting effect and opens up all sorts of possibilities for combining shapes and colour. We've used two equilateral triangles for these Egyptian-inspired earrings, but there is no reason to stop with just two layers.

Tools & Materials

8 x 3.4 mm drop beads Matt Khaki Iris (**A**)

1 g size 11 cylinder beads Matt Gold (**B**)

1 g size 11 cylinder beads Transparent Chartreuse Lustre (**C**)

1 g size 11 cylinder beads Silver-lined Olive (**D**)

2 g size 11 cylinder beads Olive Gold Matt (**E**)

2 x 14 x size 15 seed beads Olive Gold Matt (**F**)

- Nylon beading thread
- Size 12 beading needle
- Chain-nose pliers
- 2 x ear wires
- Nylon thread

Height: 3 cm (1¼ in)
Width: 3 cm (1¼ in)

Step 1 Make 4 triangles using the method on page 111 as follows: Triangle 1 x 2 using B beads for the herringbone stacks and colours C, D and E for the peyote-stitch sides; triangle 2 x 2 using C beads for the herringbone stacks and E for the 3 peyote-stitch sides (**fig. 1**). Leave a 20-cm (8-in) tail thread and finish with the working thread coming out of the top point of each triangle.

ADD THE DROP BEADS
Step 2 For each triangle, rethread the needle with the tail thread and weave this from the centre out to the left-hand point, emerging from 1 cylinder bead. Pick up 1A and pass the thread down through the other cylinder bead of the point (B or E). Weave the thread through to the right-hand point and pick up and weave in the 2nd A (**fig. 2**). Weave in the end to secure.

ADD THE LOOP TO TRIANGLE 1
Step 3 Using the working thread, making sure it is positioned emerging from 1 cylinder bead at the top point of the triangle (B or E), pick up 7F and make a loop by passing the thread back down

through the opposite cylinder bead in the point (**fig. 3**). Pass the thread through the beads again and if possible a 3rd time, but take care not to break a bead by forcing the needle through. Secure the end. Repeat for the 2nd triangle.

JOIN TRIANGLES 1 & 2
Step 4 Work with the back of the earring uppermost. Position Triangle 2 on top and about 4 cylinder beads (B) below the top of Triangle 1. Use the herringbone stack for guidance. With the working thread coming out of the top left-hand cylinder bead (E) of Triangle 2, pass the thread up through the 4th cylinder bead (B) in the herringbone stack of Triangle 1 and down through the

1 next to it. Repeat once more to secure. You may need to place 1 stitch of thread at either X to keep both triangles flat (**fig. 4**).

Step 5 With a pair of chain-nose pliers, open the wire loop at the base of the ear wires and slip through the beaded loop at the top of each earring (**fig. 5**).

TIP
Ideally these earrings should face forwards; depending on your choice of ear wire, you may need to add a jump ring to the bead loop before joining them together.

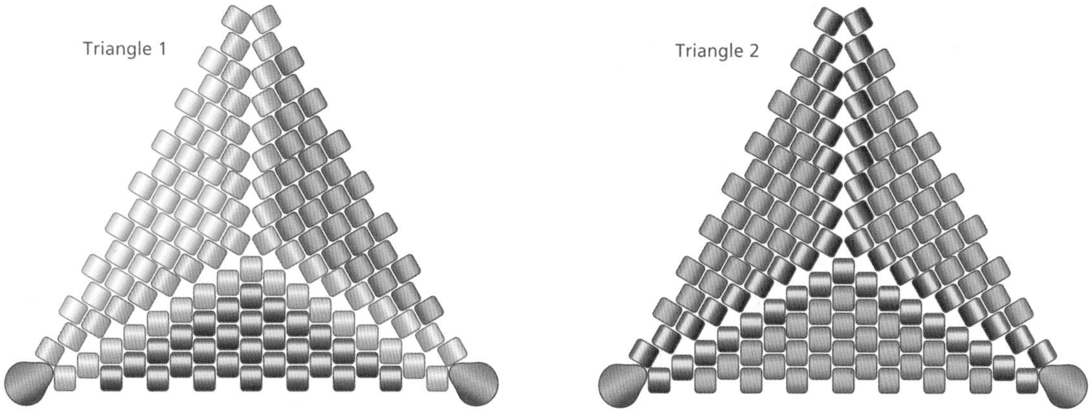

Triangle 1

Triangle 2

Fig. 1

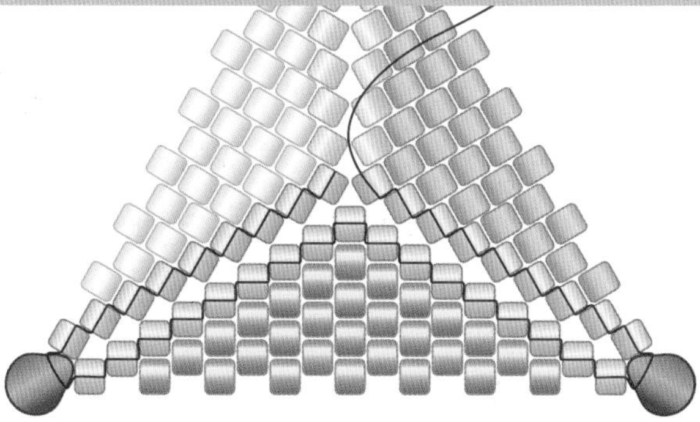

Fig. 2

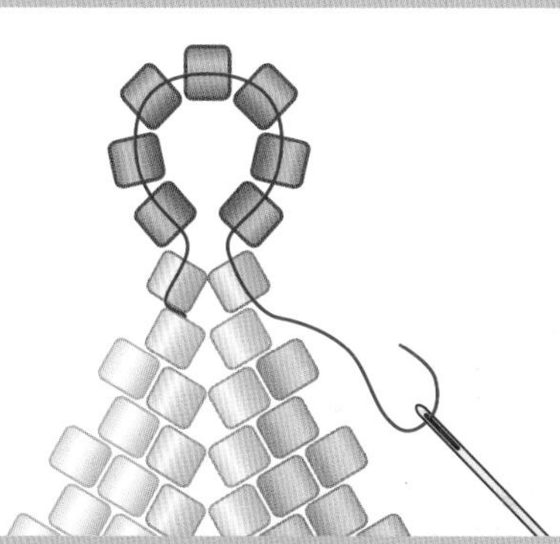

Fig. 3

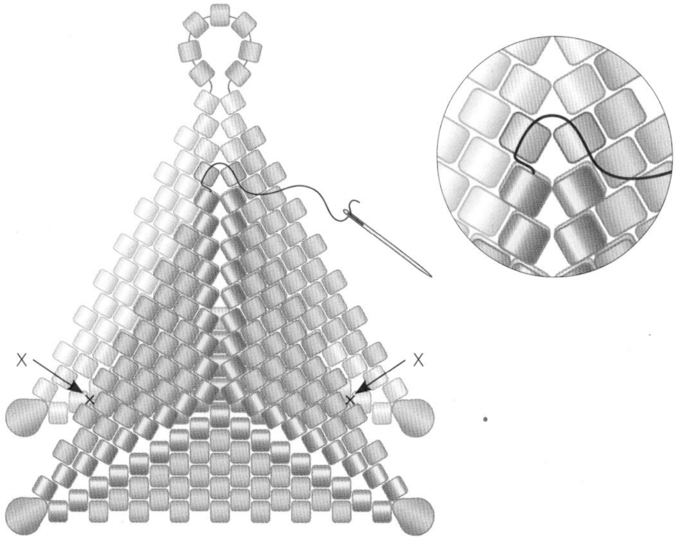

Fig. 4

X

X

X

X

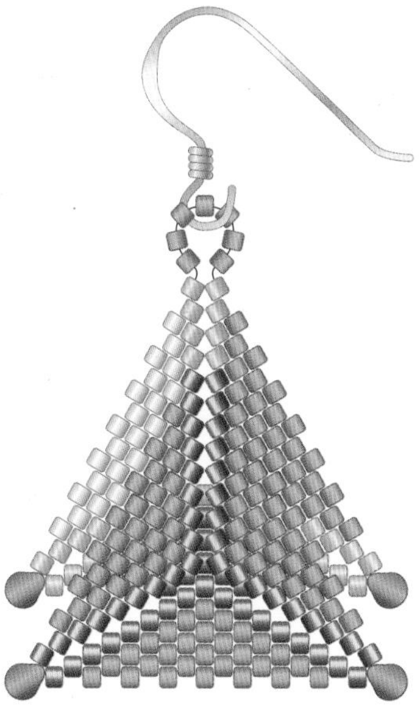

Fig. 5

12 Frills and Furbelows

Embellishing finished work can make all the difference to a design as well as helping to reinforce a piece of delicate beadwork. It can change the shape, and even hide the odd mistake or two (but don't tell anyone).

Tools & Materials

- 4 mm cube beads
- Size 8 seed beads in 2 different colours
- Size 11 seed beads
- Drop beads or magatamas
- Size 10 beading needle
- Beading thread
- Embroidery scissors

A decorative element is often just a pretty addition to the design. But sometimes, embellishing techniques also help the thread path. Making a picot turn not only leaves a three-bead edge, it also hides an otherwise clumsy 360-degree turn in the thread path. Fringing adds length, and stitching in the ditch can change the shape of a flat piece of peyote stitch.

Most fringes, frills and other furbelows are best worked using an odd number of beads; this ensures any turn beads, drops or focal beads are always centred.

Start an embellishment with a new length of stretched thread. This prevents the entire piece of beadwork from unravelling if a frill is damaged.

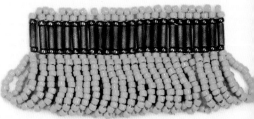

GOLDEN GLAMOUR, *Amy Severino*

A pair of peyote-stitch diamond shapes are finished off with a dramatic flourish. A fringing with lots of gold cylinder beads and bicone crystals creates a lovely rich cascade, worked off the peyote-stitch centre of each earring.

TYPES OF FRILLS AND FURBELOWS

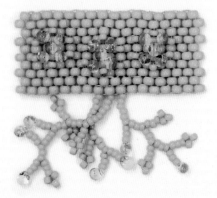

A band of peyote stitch decorated with stitch-in-the-ditch flowers and coral fronds. The flowers and fronds use green drop beads and size 11 seed beads.

Peyote stitch embellished with fringe made using size 11 seed beads and 4 mm bicone crystals with a size 15 turn bead on the end of each frond.

A ladder-stitch strip of bugles topped and tailed with size 11 seed beads has been embellished with loops and topped off with a picot edging. Note the thread passes back through the 1st bead of the loop before going up through the ladder. Each picot shares a bead with the picot before it.

FRINGING

Stitches that leave the holes of the edge beads exposed are perfect for a spot of fringing. Square stitch, loom work, herringbone and brick stitches all provide excellent canvases for a fringe detail.

STEP 1

Bring the working thread out of the first bead on the edge you want to decorate. Leave a tail of at least 15 cm (6 in) to weave in when you have finished.

STEP 2

Pick up a number of beads corresponding to the length of the fringe plus a turn bead. Take the beads down the thread to meet the edge of the beadwork. Skip the turn bead and pass back through the rest of the beads on the thread, keeping a hold on the turn bead as you draw the thread through to maintain a good tension.

Turn bead

STEP 3

Where you go next depends on the width of your beadwork. In this example, the thread passes through the cube beads and out of the other side, ready to go back down the next row to repeat.

TIP

On a piece of beadwork wider than the one shown, thread through a few beads in the body of the work before reversing back to the edge. Vary the number of beads in from the edge on each turn to avoid a ridge of thread.

To create vertical fringing, use the same technique of threading beads and turn bead but bring the thread out between beads in the beadworked base.

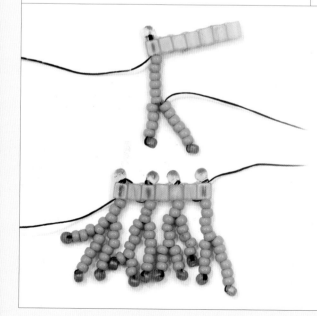

ADD DEPTH TO A FRINGE BY CREATING BRANCHES ON EACH FRINGE

Start the fringe as before, using more beads before adding the turn bead. Pass the thread back through 4 of the beads before picking up more beads and a turn bead. Pass back through all but the new turn bead, up through the remaining beads to the body of the beadwork. Repeat along the edges of the beadwork. Here drop beads have been added along the top edge as turn beads on a strip of ladder-stitched cubes to hide some of the thread. This technique can either be worked with random numbers of beads making up the branches or in a regular pattern. Sometimes known as coral stitch, this technique can also be used, combined with a picot turn to make striking beaded patterns that look like... coral.

PICOT EDGING

Three-bead picots don't always have to be used for edging. They make a nice focal point at the end of a fringe, turn in a piece of netting stitch or can be used at the end of a leaf shape such as the one on page 76.

STEP 1

Bring the working thread out of the first bead on the edge you want to decorate. Leave a tail of at least 15 cm (6 in) to weave in when you have finished.

STEP 2

Pick up 1 seed bead, 1 drop bead and 1 seed bead, and pass the needle back through the bead it has just emerged from.

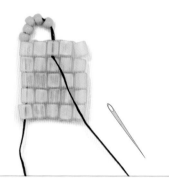

STEP 3

Work along the edge of the beadwork, adding a picot every bead, or every other bead.

Pass the thread back down through this bead

LOOPED EDGING

A row of loops using three or five beads finishes off the otherwise plain edging of a piece of loom work or brick stitch. Longer loops can add length to beadwork, or even be used as a stitch in its own right (see over the page).

STEP 1

Bring the working thread out of the first bead on the edge you want to decorate. Leave a tail of at least 15 cm (6 in) to weave in when you have finished.

STEP 2

Pick up an odd number of beads (5 here), skip over 1 edge bead and pass down through the next edge bead.

STEP 3

Pass the needle back up through the edge bead skipped over in step 2 and pick up the same number of beads as before.

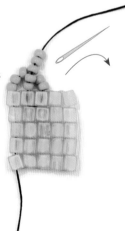

STEP 4

Repeat steps 2 and 3 along the length of the edge.

TIP

Longer loops create a different effect; here, added to a band of ladder stitch, they start to form a necklace in their own right.

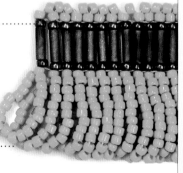

STITCH IN THE DITCH

'Stitch in the ditch' is a term used by quilters that perfectly describes filling in the gap between beads in peyote and other stitches. Used in a single line around the outer edges of a peyote bezel it adds detail (see Santa Fe Pendant on page 102), but a block of stitched ditches produces a very pleasing curve (see the doodle stitch on page 39).

STEP 1

Leaving a tail of at least 15 cm (6 in) to weave in when you have finished, pass the working thread through the first bead of the row you want to decorate. Pick up a bead and pass the needle through the next bead in the row, skipping over the ditch.

STEP 2

Continue working your way along to the end of the row. To anchor the last bead, pass the needle under the horizontal thread on the outer edge before passing it through the 1st bead in the next row.

STEP 3

Continue to add beads into each ditch, pulling on the thread to keep a fairly tight tension. As you bead, the work will curl around. How much the work curls depends on the beads you use and how much surface is covered.

TIP

Try the technique using smaller beads or drop beads, or experiment with dotting beads around rather than on every row.

DESIGNER: KAREN WILKINSON

Length (including clasp):
21 cm (8¼ in)

Loop the Loop Bracelet

This simple fringing technique illustrates perfectly how switching the materials can completely change the look of a piece of beadwork. We've used a 'soup' mix of seed beads, magatamas and drops, but try using 4 mm glass pearls, crystals or fire-polished Czech glass beads for a sparkly version. If you're a fan of a random look, ignore the bead sequence for the loops and pick up the beads as they come to hand.

Tools & Materials

- Approx. 30 g mix of size 8 and 6 seed beads, magatamas and drops or similar in coordinating colours
- 1 x 10 mm focal bead for clasp
- 1 x size 11 seed bead for clasp
- Beading thread (nylon or braided monofilament if your mix includes crystals)
- Conditioning wax
- Size 10 needle
- Stop bead

Step 1 Thread the needle with 2 wingspans of lightly conditioned thread. Add a stop bead, leaving a 32-cm (14-in) tail. Pick up and string enough size 8 beads to make the core long enough to fit comfortably around your wrist, less 2.5 cm (1 in) for the clasp **(fig. 1)**.

Step 2 Pick up 20 size 8 beads (or enough to fit around the focal bead) for the loop end of the clasp. Pass the thread back through the last 4 beads of the core and do a half-hitch knot by catching the working thread around the core thread, passing the needle through the loop that

forms and drawing the thread tight. Changing direction, pass the thread back up through the 4 core beads and around the loop again. Pass the thread around the loop 3 more times **(fig. 2)**.

Step 3 Pass through the 1st core bead and pick up 7 beads in the following loop sequence: *1 seed bead, 1 magatama, 1 seed bead, 1 pearl or crystal, 1 seed bead, 1 magatama, 1 seed bead* **(fig. 3)**. Pass the thread through the next bead in the core **(fig. 4)**. Continue to add loops between each size 8 bead until the last bead in the core **(fig. 5)**.

Step 4 To add the focal-bead clasp, pick up 3 core beads, the focal bead, 1 core bead and 1 size 11 bead. Pass the thread back through the core and focal beads and 3 core beads **(fig. 6)**. Do a half-hitch knot to change the direction of the thread and go back up through the 3 core beads, focal and size 11 bead and back down through the core beads until the focal bead feels secure (see step 2). Weave the end in and trim.

STEP-BY-STEP DIAGRAMS

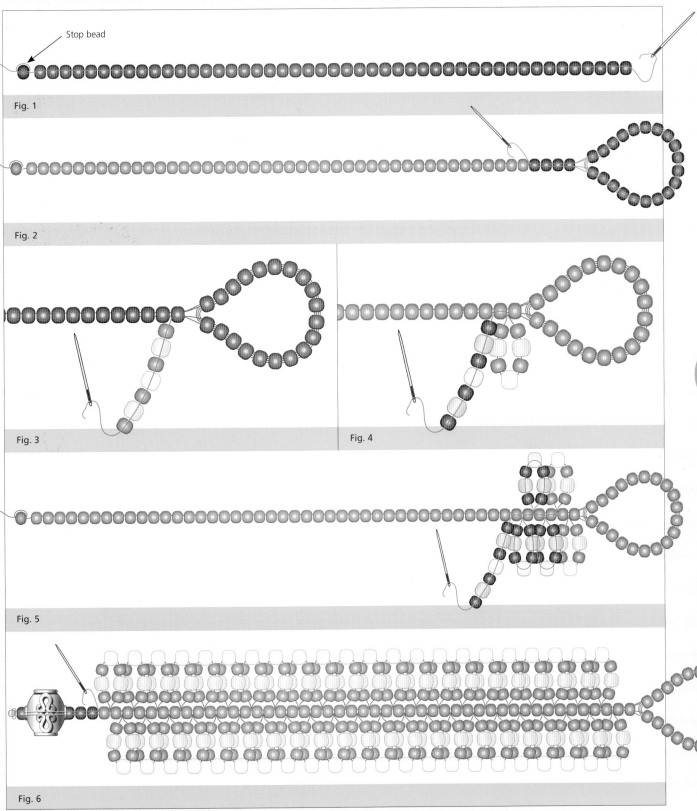

Stop bead

Fig. 1

Fig. 2

Fig. 3

Fig. 4

Fig. 5

Fig. 6

13 Beadweaving on a Loom

Weaving with thread has been around for almost as long as humankind has worn clothing – beadweaving on a loom has more recent origins but is still an art with a venerable history and has always excited anyone with a passion for seed beads. What doesn't always excite is the weaving in of the warp threads at the end of a project. Sometimes there are ways around that and sometimes not, but the end result is worth the effort.

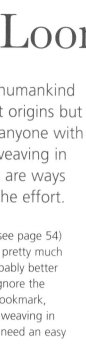

Tools & Materials

- Loom
- Bead mat
- Size 8 seed beads
- Size 10 beading needle
- New reel of beading thread
- Embroidery scissors
- Masking tape (optional)
- Focal bead (optional)
- 2 x calottes (optional)
- Clasp (optional)
- Clear nail varnish (optional)

Loomed beadwork looks very much like square stitch (see page 54) to the naked eye and patterns for either technique are pretty much interchangeable. In fact, if the project is small, it is probably better to work it in square stitch. But do not be tempted to ignore the loom – it is possible to whip up a strip of fabric for a bookmark, a bracelet or even a belt in a relatively short time. And weaving in the ends can be done at the end of the day when you need an easy project to relax with.

On these pages you will find the techniques for getting started on a basic, inexpensive loom. Once you get the bug, you can always upgrade to a sturdier, larger model.

LOOMED GUMLEAF CUFF, *Caron Reid*

This cuff, which is a reflection on Australian flora, has been cleverly extended at the sides with brick stitch to make the leaves break out of the confines of the loom-worked rectangle. The beaded edging even stops to allow the leaves to create an interesting perspective effect.

TYPES OF LOOMED BEADWORK

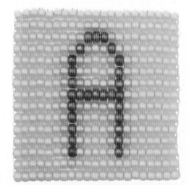

The letter A followed from a cross-stitch chart using size 8 seed beads.

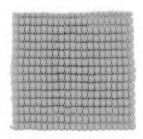

Loom work makes light work of producing patterns and pictures in beadwork, as long as you don't mind weaving in the warp threads afterwards. Size 11 seed beads were used here.

Size 11 cylinder beads need a tight tension to begin with to pull the warp threads closer together, but all three swatches were made on the same basic loom.

THREADING A LOOM: INDIVIDUAL WARPS METHOD

Most looms come with a set of instructions specific to the model, but the set-up principles will be the same. Individual warps take longer to set up and need securing or weaving in at the end.

STEP 1

Cut 1 more 63.5-cm (25-in) thread than the number of beads you plan to use (i.e. 10 beads = 11 warp threads), stretching the thread as you unspool it from the reel. Tie together in a simple knot and position either side of the peg at the end of the loom furthest away from you.

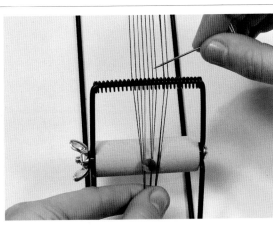

STEP 2

Using the beading or a tapestry needle in one hand and applying gentle tension on the threads with the other, ease the warps into place on the end spring. Place the outer warps first and work inwards to the centre.

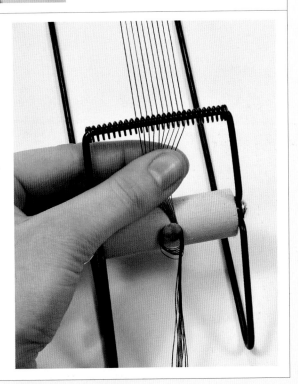

STEP 3

Place the warps in the corresponding grooves at the other end of the loom and secure with a knot around the peg. You can adjust any slipped warps at this point and then tighten them slightly by turning the bar with the peg slightly towards you. There should be some tension in the warps, but not so much that you could play a tune on them.

THREADING A LOOM: CONTINUOUS WARPS OR PULLED WARP METHOD

This method is quicker to set up, but drawing the threads through at the end can be tricky over a large piece of beadwork.

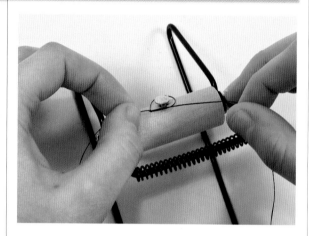

STEP 1

Start with a new reel of thread and unspool several feet, stretching it as you do so. Tie the end of the thread around the peg furthest away from you with a simple knot or slip knot. To centre your work on the loom, find the central notch on the spring and count half the number of total warps out to the left-hand side to find the right notch for your first warp thread.

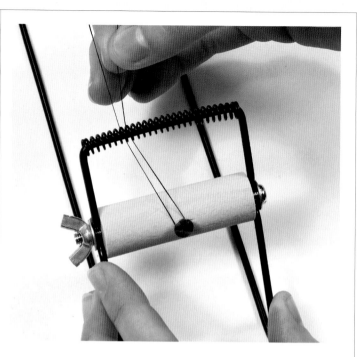

STEP 2

Take the thread down to the corresponding notch and around the peg, from left to right, then up again to the top peg. Continue back down, then up, fitting the thread into the notches, always winding around the pegs from left to right.

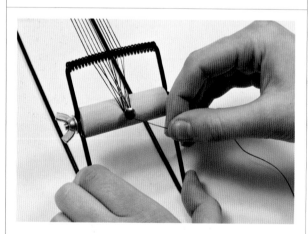

STEP 3

Continue until you have 1 more warp thread than number of beads and fasten the thread around the bottom peg with a knot or piece of masking tape before cutting. Make sure all the warps are correctly placed and the tension suitably adjusted (see step 3, page 123).

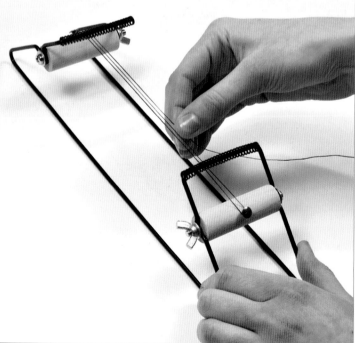

WEAVING ON THE LOOM, BOTH WARP METHODS

Once you have set up the warp thread by either method, the process of weaving the beads on the loom is the same. It is best to place smaller looms on a bead mat to hold the loom and beads steady as you work.

STEP 2

Take the needle and weft thread under the warps to the right-hand side of the loom and pick up 10 beads on the needle.

STEP 1

Thread a size 10 beading needle with approximately one and a half wingspans of stretched thread. Leaving approximately 20 cm (8 in), anchor the tail with an overhand knot around the left-hand arm of the loom, just below the wooden roller. You can use masking tape if you'd rather avoid a knot. This is the weft thread.

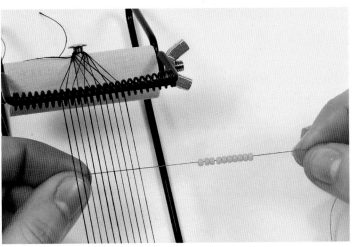

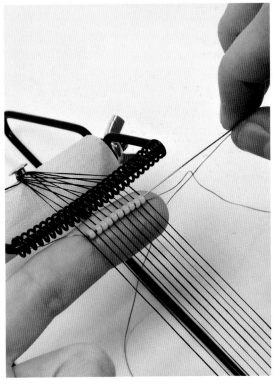

STEP 3

Slide the beads down the weft thread. Starting at the end of the loom furthest from you, come up from below the warps and position a bead between each one, making sure there is a warp thread either side of the outside edge beads.

STEP 4

Pass the needle through each bead from right to left over the top of the warp threads and draw the weft through so that it is looped around the warp on the right-hand edge. The first row can be fiddly, so if necessary, thread through the beads a few at a time, always starting from the right-hand side.

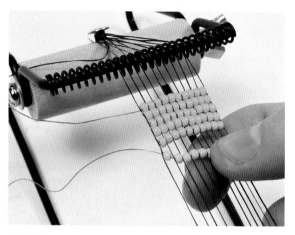

STEP 5

Continue to add rows from right to left, keeping an even, relaxed tension throughout. Every few rows, check that none of the threads have been accidentally pierced by sliding a row gently up and down the warp. This is particularly important if you have used the continuous warp method to start.

INCREASING AND DECREASING

If your design calls for increasing on either edge, remember to set up enough warp threads to accommodate the extra bead(s) at the start.

INCREASING

Starting at the left-hand side of the loom, wrap the weft thread around the outer warp thread of the existing work to anchor it. Make sure the thread is coming out towards you, between the old and the new warp. Pick up a bead and position it at what is now the beginning of the next row. Bring the needle out under the new outer warp thread and go back through the new bead. Finish the row by picking up and weaving beads in the usual way. To increase at the right-hand edge, just add an extra bead to the needle.

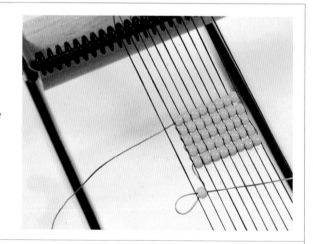

DECREASING

At the left-hand edge, pass the needle around and under the outer warp thread and back through the first bead of the row just added. Anchor the weft thread around the new outer warp thread ready to start the new row and pick up the beads in the usual way (not illustrated). To decrease at the right-hand edge, add 1 fewer bead and loop around the new outer warp thread before passing back through the beads (see left).

FINISHING OFF: REMOVING AND FINISHING INDIVIDUAL WARPS

Think of the ends as an opportunity to add fringing or clasps. But don't leave them loose or the beadwork could come undone.

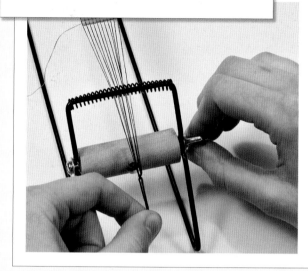

Loosen a roller at one end of the loom (left) and slip the knotted warps off both pegs and untie the knots (right). Straighten out the warp threads ready for finishing. The simplest way to finish off is to fold the warp threads behind the work and sew on a backing fabric to hide all the ends. The tidier method is to weave each of the warp threads back through the work. Try to vary the thread path as you weave the ends back in to keep the weave flat. Weaving in the ends also gives you the option of adding clasps or decorative fringing to the ends first.

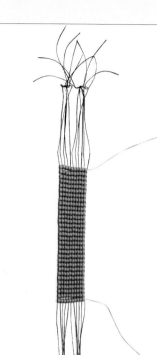

FINISHING OFF: MAKING A LOOP FASTENING

Take advantage of the long threads to add more beads in the shape of a loop or two to go around a corresponding focal-bead toggle for an effective finish to a woven cuff.

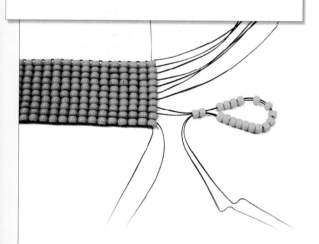

Choose either the 2 centre warp threads or 2 that correspond to the position of the toggle(s) at the other end and thread on enough beads to fit over the opposite focal bead plus 2. Pass the needle back down through the plus 2 beads to make a loop. Remove the needle to separate the 2 threads and weave them back through the work 1 at a time.

FINISHING OFF: MAKING FRINGING OR A TOGGLE FASTENING

A loop needs a toggle at the other end if the beadwork is to be a bracelet. Or just embellish the ends with seed-bead fringing.

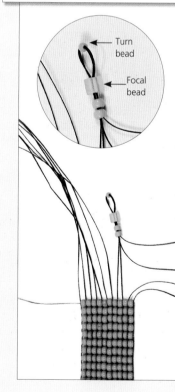

Turn bead

Focal bead

In much the same way as you made the loop fastening (left), you can add fringing or a toggle clasp. For fringing using 1 or 2 warp threads, pick up a group of beads, making sure you start and end with the smaller turn beads. Skipping the bead nearest the needle, pass the thread down through the remaining beads and weave the ends back into the work. For a toggle, use the same method but add a focal bead before the last seed bead.

FINISHING OFF: ADDING A CLASP

You can thread calottes on to the tails of warp threads to join on to metal clasps if you prefer those to beaded ones.

STEP 1

Starting at the outer edges, weave each of the warp ends in toward the centre until all the ends are coming out of the middle of the work, or either side of the middle bead if there is an odd number.

STEP 2

Slip a calotte down over the threads, cup side facing away from the work, and tie a knot in the warps to secure the calotte. I use 2 overhand knots. A top tip is to thickly brush the knot and threads with clear nail varnish at this stage and leave to completely dry before trimming the ends. The calotte is then ready to be closed and a fastening of your choice added. For a simpler finish, separate the warp threads into groups of 3 and braid them, finishing off with a neat knot. Use these braids to fasten the cuff.

FINISHING OFF: REMOVING AND FINISHING CONTINUOUS WARP THREADS

Patience and persistence are needed to remove the threads, starting from the centre. Use a finger to stop the beads bunching up as you pull (see step 2).

STEP 1

Loosen 1 of the rollers as before and carefully lift the looped warps off the pegs. Don't forget the first end will have been knotted on and will need untying or cutting. Straighten out and separate the looped warps.

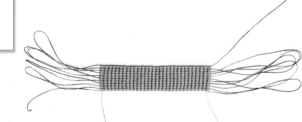

STEP 2

Gently pull on 1 of the central loops and draw the warp through the work.

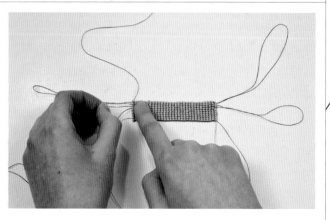

STEP 3

Continue to pull each loop in this way, taking care to keep the beads flat. Small lines of thread will be visible at either end of the work.

DESIGNER: MARY MARSHALL

Harlequin Bookmark

Working with a basic loom does not mean having to create basic beadwork. We used the most available loom on the market to make this shaped bookmark. Our version is worked in cylinder beads to create a smooth, even finish, but any size 11 seed bead will work. Try to match the thread colour to the beads on the outer edges, since it is slightly visible.

Tools & Materials

- Size 11 cylinder beads in 5 colours

  Matt Metallic Bronze x 459 (**A**)

  Matt Metallic Olive Gold x 330 (**B**)

  Blue Zircon Silver Lined x 137 (**C**)

  Silver Lined Pale Cream x 124 (**D**)

  Opaque Old Rose Lustre x 124 (**E**)

- Small loom
- Nylon beading thread such as S-Lon or Nymo
- Size 10 beading needle
- Size 12 beading needle
- Ruler
- Thread Zapper (optional)

Step 1 Thread the loom with 16 individual warp threads, thread the size 10 beading needle and anchor this weft thread following the instructions on page 123.

Step 2 Reading the chart from top left (X) to right, pick up the beads in the same order. You'll find it easier to follow the chart if you place a ruler under each row as you work down. Check each row against the chart before

you start the next one to avoid discovering any mistakes when it's too late to fix them.

Step 3 Shape the point by decreasing 1 stitch at either end of the next 7 rows, until only 1 bead is left. Loosen the loom rollers and remove the work from the pegs. Weave in the ends using the size 12 needle. A Thread Zapper is helpful here to tidy up and secure any tiny threads.

Length: 13.5 cm (5¼ in)
Width: 2 cm (¾ in)

TIP
Cylinder beads are generally smaller than the gap between the warp threads on a basic loom, so after you have woven 2 or 3 rows, gently tighten the weft to draw the beads into each other.

CHAPTER 3

Guest designer projects

This chapter features projects specially created by five renowned designers from across the world. Each project uses techniques from the book to show you how the building blocks of beadweaving can create exquisite works of wearable art. The instructions refer back to the step-by-step pages where applicable and user-friendly diagrams guide you through the beading process.

DESIGNER: NANCY DALE

Ribbons and Rows Bracelet

This is a lovely cuff bracelet that frames crystals and pearls for a dramatic look. Make one with only one row of embellishment for a perfect everyday bracelet, or make a larger four-, five- or six-row cuff for a real statement piece.

Tools & Materials

- 14 g size 11 seed beads – Matt Light Lilac Toho #766 (**A**)

- 2 g size 15 seed beads – Silver Plated Toho #714 (**B**)

- 54 x 4 mm Swarovski Crystal Bicones – Light Amethyst AB (**C**)

- 26 x 3–3.5 mm Freshwater Pearls – Golden Cream (**D**)

- 1 x 4-loop sterling silver sliding-tube clasp
- 0.12 mm Fireline Thread – Crystal
- Size 12 beading needle

Length (including clasp): 16.5 cm (6½ in)

Width: 2.5 cm (1 in)

Step 1 Begin by making 4 CRAW ropes (see page 80), each one 54 units (cubes) long. Leave the ends.

Step 2 Lay 2 of the ropes side by side, making sure that they are not twisted and that the first cubes from each rope are aligned. On rope 1, pass the needle through the side bead nearest rope 2 so that it is emerging at bead 1 (**fig. 1**).

Step 3 Using RAW (see page 79), connect your ropes together with new units as follows (**fig. 1**):
a) Pick up 1A and pass up through the corresponding bead on the right-hand rope.
b) Pick up 1A and go down through the bead you exited in step 3a.
c) Pass through the A added in step 3b. This makes 1 RAW unit.

Step 4 a) Pass down through the next side bead on the right-hand rope.
b) Pick up 1A and pass up through the corresponding side bead on the left-hand rope.
c) Pass through the A you started from in step 3c, down the side bead on the right-hand rope and through the A added in step 4b.

Step 5 a) Pass down through the next side bead of the left-hand rope.

b) Pick up 1A and pass up through the corresponding side bead on the right-hand rope.
c) Pass through the A added in step 4b, the side bead on the left-hand rope and the A added in step 5b.

Step 6 Continue following steps 4 and 5 until you have connected the 2 ropes with new RAW units. Keep checking as you go to make sure that the rope is straight and untwisted (**fig. 2**).

ABOUT THE DESIGNER ● Nancy is a long-time beader and self-confessed beadaholic. She sells her creations online at Etsy and works mainly in off-loom stitches.

STEP-BY-STEP DIAGRAMS

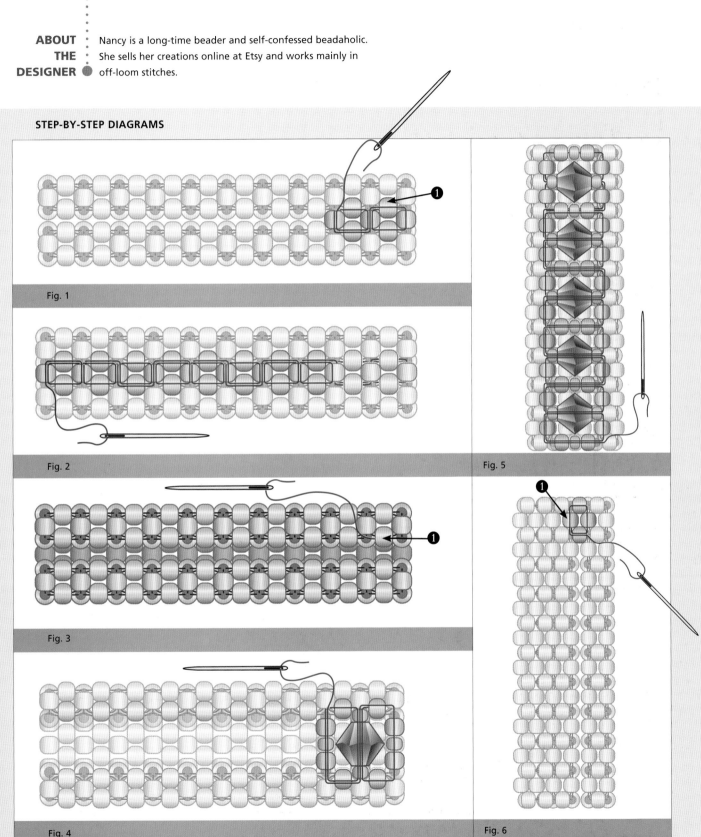

Fig. 1

Fig. 2

Fig. 3

Fig. 4

Fig. 5

Fig. 6

DESIGNER: NANCY DALE

Step 7 Once both ropes are connected, turn the work over – the side you've just connected will be the back of the bracelet. You now have a channel between the 2 ropes on the front side.

Step 8 On rope 2, pass the needle through the inner side bead so that it is emerging at bead 1 (**fig. 3**). You are now ready to embellish the front of the bracelet by connecting the front of the ropes with RAW.

Step 9 a) Pick up 1B, 1C, 1B and go up through the corresponding side bead on the right-hand rope.
b) Pick up 1A, 1B, 1A and go down through the side bead you started from in step 9a.
c) Pass through the B, C, B added in step 9a, and down through the next side bead on the right-hand rope.

Step 10 a) Pick up 1A, 1B, 1A and pass up through the corresponding side bead on the left-hand rope.
b) Pass through the B, C, B you added in step 9a and the side bead you started from in this step.
c) Pass through the A, B, A added in step 10a, and down through the next side bead on the left-hand rope, thus adding a RAW unit with 3 beads for the top and bottom (**fig. 4**).

Step 11 a) Pick up 1B, 1C, 1B and pass up through the corresponding side bead on the right-hand rope, through the A, B, A added in step 10a and down through the side bead you started from in this step.
b) Pass through the B, C, B you added in step 11a, and down through the next side bead on the right-hand rope.

Step 12 Repeat steps 10–11 to connect your ropes all the way down their length; you should add a total of 27C and end with 1A, 1B, 1A (**fig. 5**).

Step 13 Turn your work over so that you're looking at the back of it. Lay the third length of rope down next to 1 side, and follow steps 3–8 to connect the next section (**fig. 6**).

Step 14 Starting with the thread emerging from bead 1 in **fig. 7**, pick up 1A, 1B, 1A and go up through the corresponding side bead on the right-hand rope,

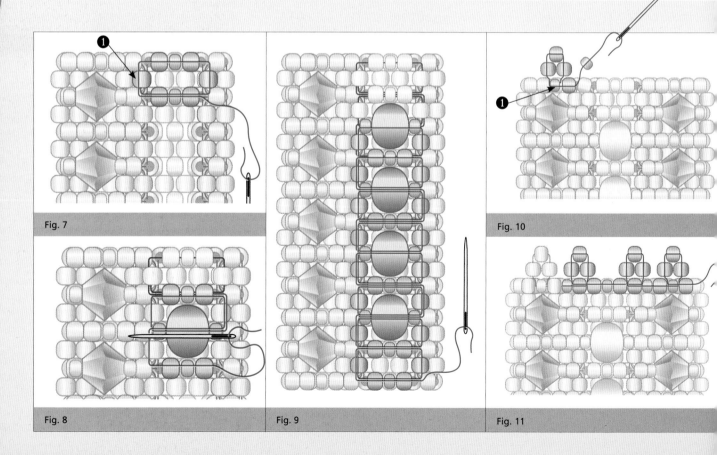

Fig. 7

Fig. 8

Fig. 9

Fig. 10

Fig. 11

then pick up 1A, 1B, 1A and go down through bead 1 again. Pass through the first A, B, A added in this step and down through the next side bead on the right-hand rope (**fig. 7**).

Step 15 a) Pick up 1B, 1D, 1B and pass up through the corresponding side bead on the left-hand rope.
b) Pass through the last A, B, A you added and the side bead you started from in step 15a.
c) Pass through the B, D, B just added and down through the next side bead on the left-hand rope (**fig. 8**).

Step 16 Pick up 1A, 1B, 1A and pass up through the corresponding side bead on the right-hand rope, through the B, D, B added in step 15a and down through the side bead you started from in this step.

Step 17 Continue to alternate steps 15–16 down the rope to add 26D and end with A, B, A for the last 2 stitches (**fig. 9**).

Step 18 For your final rope, follow steps 3–12 with the same colour sequence, connecting the back of the ropes and then the front to add another 27C and

beginning and ending with A, B, A for the last two stitches.

Step 19 Thread the needle with a wingspan of new thread and position it so that the thread emerges from bead 1 in **fig. 10**, ready to add 4 RAW units on the front side and 4 RAW units on the reverse side; the clasp loops will be sandwiched between these units.

Step 20 Pick up 3A, and pass through bead 1, to make 1 RAW unit. Pass through the next A. Pick up 1B and pass through the next A (**fig. 10**).

Step 21 Pick up 3A and pass through the A you exited again to make 1 RAW unit. Pick up 1B and pass down through the A, B, A.

Step 22 Pick up 1B and pass down through the next A. Pick up 3A and pass through the A you exited to make 1 RAW unit.

Step 23 Pick up 1B and pass down through the next A and B. Pick up 3A and pass through the B to make 1 RAW unit and then down through the next A (**fig. 11**).

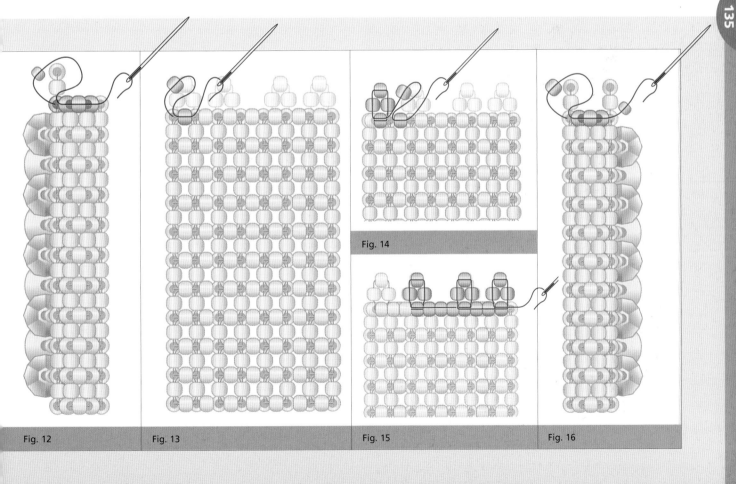

Fig. 12

Fig. 13

Fig. 14

Fig. 15

Fig. 16

DESIGNER: NANCY DALE

Step 24 Pick up 1B and pass through the top 3A on your rope to exit from the back side of the bracelet (**fig. 12**).

Step 25 Pick up 1A and pass through the next A (**fig. 13**).

Step 26 Pick up 3A and pass through the A you exited to make 1 RAW unit. Pick up 1A and pass down through the next A (**fig. 14**).

Step 27 Pick up 3A and pass through the A you exited to make 1 RAW unit. Pick up 1A and pass down through the next A twice.

Step 28 Pick up 3A and pass through the A you exited to make 1 RAW unit. Pick up 1A and pass down through the next A.

Step 29 Pick up 3A and pass down through the A you exited to make the last RAW unit (**fig. 15**). Pick up 1A and pass down through the next A, then pass through the next top 3A on your rope to exit the front of the bracelet again (**fig. 16**).

Step 30 Pick up 1B and pass through the top A and B (**fig. 17**).

Step 31 Weave through the RAW unit to exit the top bead; your thread will be exiting up and away from the work. To attach the clasp, circle stitch the 2 point beads from the front and back RAW units together, sandwiching the clasp loop between them. Place your clasp at the edge of your work, with the first clasp loop between the front and back RAW units.

Step 32 Pass down through the clasp loop (**fig. 18**).

Step 33 Pass through the back RAW unit point bead. Pass

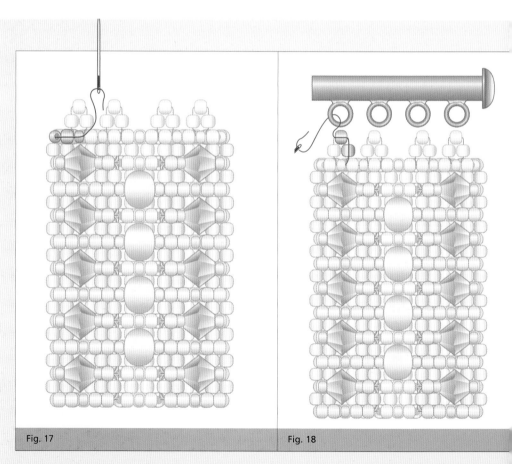

Fig. 17
Fig. 18

back up through the clasp loop (**fig. 19**).

Step 34 Pass through the front top bead to exit in the same direction you started from. Reinforce this stitch again.

Step 35 Weave over to the top bead on the next RAW unit and repeat steps 31–34 to attach the remaining clasp loops. Weave in and end your thread (**fig. 20**).

Step 36 Repeat steps 19–35 to attach the other half of your clasp to the opposite end of the bracelet.

TIP
Sizing: Seven units equals approximately 2.5 cm (1 in), but they do compact and shrink a little as you add the embellishments, so overestimate if changing the size.

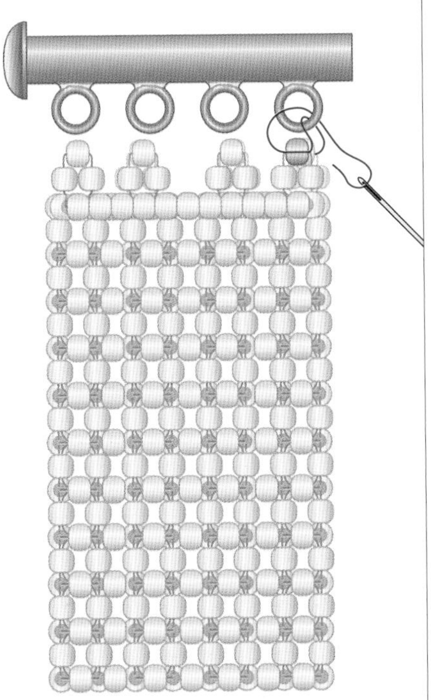

Fig. 19

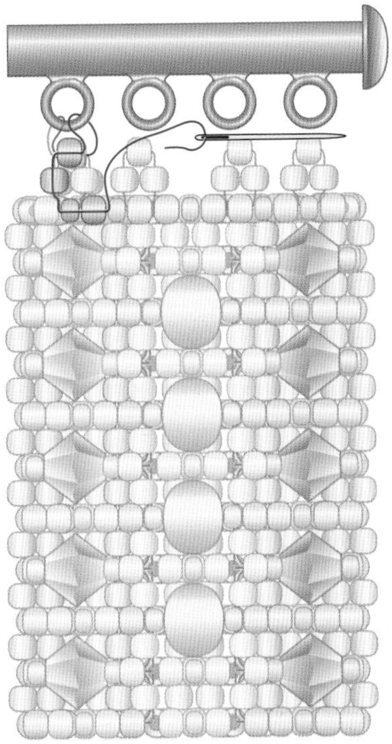

Fig. 20

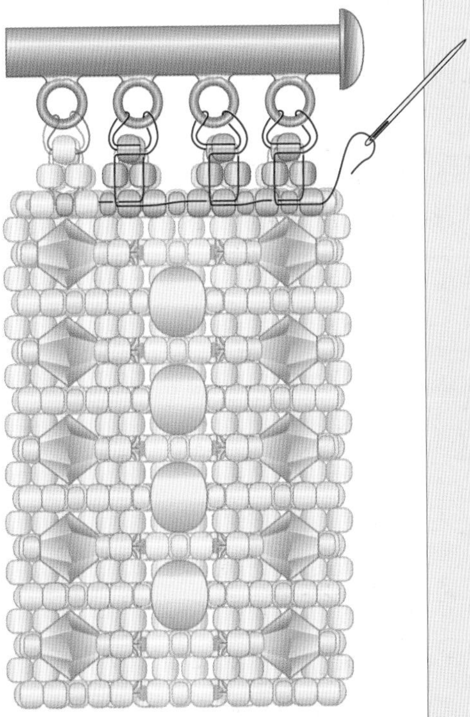

Fig. 21

DESIGNER: HEATHER COLLIN

Nefertiti Necklace

In this design, you will be shown how to create a framework of CRAW off from the side of the beadwork and connecting two sections to create interesting shapes. Just these two techniques within CRAW will open up a whole new world of ideas for beaders.

Tools & Materials

- For 1 pendant
- 7 g size 8 Matt Bronze or Matt Khaki mix Miyuki seed beads (**A**)
- 2 g size 11 Blue Zircon or Galvanised Magenta Miyuki seed beads (**B**)
- 3 g size 12 Gold Toho
- 3-cut metal beads or 2 g size 11 gold seed beads (**C**)
- 1 x 8 mm Chocolate Brown or Magenta round glass beads
- (6) 4 x 7 mm bronze spikes
- Nylon beading thread
- Conditioning wax
- Size 12 beading needle
- Scissors
- Medium-link bronze chain
- 1 x bronze clasp to suit

Materials for necklace

- Double up on your supplies (see page 141)
- Plus 3 medium jump rings and 2 x 12 mm focal beads

SECTION 1

Step 1 Thread the needle and string 4A on to a span of stretched and conditioned thread. Leaving a tail to work away later, pass through the beads again and exit the 1st bead strung. With A beads, work 1 CRAW cube unit (see page 80) (**fig. 1**, unit 1).

Step 2 2nd CRAW unit: pick up 1B, 1A, 1B and pass through the A just exited and the next A in the base. Pick up 1B, 1A and pass through the 1st B just added, the A just exited and the next A in the base. Continue working around the unit in CRAW, picking up 1B, 1A and, for the final pass, 1A. Each vertical bead should be an A and the horizontal bead a B (B/A/B). Work 8 more units with B/A/B beads, ending with unit 10 (**fig. 1**).

Step 3 Work 1 unit with A beads only (**fig. 2**, unit 11). Step down and exit a vertical bead on the right of the work (**fig. 2**).

Detailing the 'corners'

Note: This step will be referred to as DTC.
Step 4 String 1C and sewing in a clockwise fashion, pass through the next A. Repeat to add a total of 4C on this face of the

TIP

Winding the tail thread 5 times around the fourth finger of your non-dominant hand keeps it out of the way and helps to maintain even tension in the beadwork.

beadwork, then work needle to exit the back and repeat. Flip the work over again, working the needle to exit out the vertical A on the right-hand side of the rope, ready to add Section 2 (**fig. 3**).

SECTION 2 (WORKED AT RIGHT ANGLES TO SECTION 1)

Note: The last unit added in Section 1 (unit 11) now becomes the 1st unit of this section.
Step 5 Stitch 4 rows with B/A/B beads and then 1 row with A/A/A beads. DTC the back and front of the last unit, then exit to the right of that, ready to add Section 3 (**fig. 4**).

SECTION 3

Step 6 Bead 9 rows with B/A/B beads and 1 row with A/A/A beads. DTC the back and front of the last unit with C beads, then exit the top-left A bead (**fig. 5**).

Pendant length: 9 cm (3½ in.)
Pendant width: 2.5 cm (1 in)

Close the frame

Step 7 Connect Section 1 and Section 2 with normal RAW (see page 79), using C beads on the reverse side of the beadwork. Pass through the beads again to make a secure connection (**fig. 5a**).

Section 2

Section 1

Section 3

Section 4

Section 9

Section 5

Section 8

Section 6

Section 7

ABOUT THE DESIGNER Heather started bead stringing in 2007 and soon found she needed a greater challenge. After battling with peyote as her first stitch, she realized a passion had been born. She now has an online Etsy store.

STEP-BY-STEP DIAGRAMS

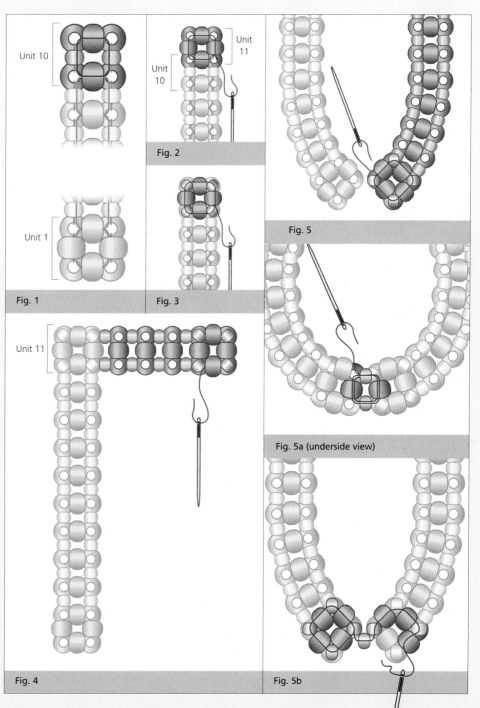

Unit 10

Unit 11

Unit 10

Fig. 2

Unit 1

Fig. 1

Fig. 3

Fig. 5

Fig. 5a (underside view)

Unit 11

Fig. 4

Fig. 5b

TIP

You are creating a flat frame – make sure that you are working off the correct set of beads.

Step 8 DTC the 1st unit of Section 1, then pass the needle through to exit to the right of the last unit in Section 3, ready to add Section 4 (**fig. 5b**).

SECTIONS 4–5

Step 9 Bead 4 rows B/A/B beads and 1 row A/A/A. DTC the back and front of the last 'unit' and exit out the top (last row of A beads).

Step 10 Bead 3 rows B/A/B beads and 1 row A/A/A. DTC the back and front of the last unit, then exit to the side.

DESIGNER: HEATHER COLLIN

SECTIONS 6–7
Step 11 Bead 5 rows B/A/B beads and 1 row A/A/A. DTC the back and front of the last unit, then exit to the side. Repeat for Section 7 (**fig. 6**).

SECTION 8: CLOSE THE FRAME
Step 12 Bead 2 rows B/A/B beads, then connect Section 8 to the 4 side A beads of Section 4 (do not sew through the C beads). See **figs 6a–6d** for detail. Pass the needle through to exit the opposite end of the detailed unit.

SECTION 9: CLOSE THE FRAME
Step 13 Bead 3 rows B/A/B beads, then connect Section 9 to the 4 side A beads of Section 1 with B beads. See **figs 6a–6d** for detail. Pass the needle through to exit the 1st connecting bead (C) added at the end of Section 3 (**fig. 6**).

ADD THE CENTRE BEAD
Step 14 String an 8 mm glass bead and sew through the opposite C bead, and back through the 8 mm bead and the C first exited. Turn the work over

and use the 2nd C added in step 7 to secure the 8 mm bead on the other side and seat it firmly in the centre of the middle 'frame'. Pass the needle through to the right and exit the first B on the inside of the upper frame (**fig. 7**).

DETAILING THE EDGES
Back inside edge
Step 15 Prepare a new thread. Refer to **fig. 8** and starting at X, add 1C per stitch between the B beads along the inner edge of the top, middle and bottom frames. Note: Do not pull the thread too

firmly when adding the C beads or the work will distort.

Back outside edge
Step 16 Work the needle to the outside edge and add 1C per stitch between the B beads of the bottom frame, 2C per stitch to the middle frame and 1C per stitch for the top frame (**fig. 8**). Pass the needle through and exit the top of the middle frame.

Front inside edge
Step 17 Repeat step 15 for the back (**fig. 8**).

STEP-BY-STEP DIAGRAMS

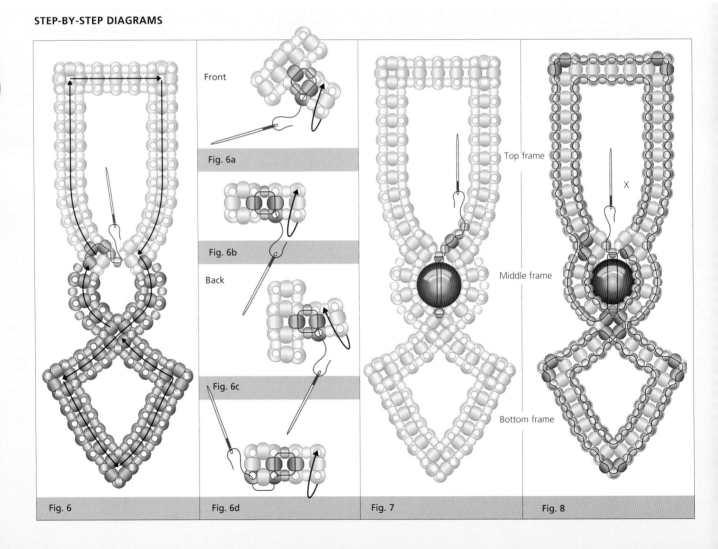

Front

Fig. 6a

Fig. 6b

Back

Fig. 6c

Fig. 6d

Top frame

Middle frame

Bottom frame

X

Fig. 6   Fig. 7   Fig. 8

Front outside edge

Step 18 Pass the needle through to the outside and add 1C per stitch between the B beads of the bottom frame (**fig. 8**).

Step 19 Add 1 spike between the B beads on the outer edge of the middle frame. Note that the spikes do not face outwards – they must be seated so that the points face downwards and the base of the spike faces you (**fig. 9**).

Step 20 Pass the needle back down the inner edge of the

middle frame and exit the 1st spike added. Add 1C between each spike (**fig. 9**).

Step 21 Add 1C per stitch for the top frame (**fig. 8**).

Step 22 Repeat steps 19 and 20 on the other side of the middle frame (**fig. 9**). Work the thread away and trim.

CHAIN TAB: ODD-COUNT PEYOTE

Start a new thread at the top of the pendant and exit the 2nd C

from the end. Add 4C beads across the top and work an odd-count peyote strip off these beads (see page 73). Make the strip about 24 rows long, checking that your chain will pass through the tab before zipping it closed (see page 103) to the row of C beads at the back of the pendant. Work the thread away and trim (**fig. 9a**).

Cut a length of chain to suit, and pass it through the tab before attaching your clasp.

CHOKER/NECKLACE DESIGN OPTION

Step 1 Bead 2 pendants.

Step 2 Insert and attach the 12 mm beads to the top frame via the 3rd bead on either side of the frame.

Step 3 Line up the pendants and connect together with C beads both at the back and the front of the pendant (**fig. 10**).

Step 4 Pass a jump ring through the centre of the detailed corners at the bottom of each pendant and link those 2 rings together with a 3rd jump ring. Create a dangle of your own choice to attach to the 3rd jump ring.

Step 5 Pass the chain through the tabs at the top of each pendant and attach a suitable clasp OR bead a thin CRAW rope with only size 11 beads to use instead of chain.

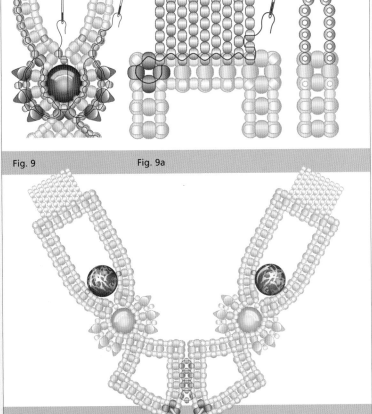

Fig. 9   Fig. 9a

Fig. 10

DESIGNER: GLENDA MAC NAUGHTON

Rosetta Bracelet

Learn to combine circular and flat herringbone, circular and flat peyote and a simple embellishment to create components that when joined form the Rosetta Bracelet. Rosetta Birks, a founder of the Women's Suffrage League of South Australia (formed in 1888), inspired the bracelet. Bead Rosetta and connect with women past and present who champion women's rights.

TIP
Work all the circular stitches in a clockwise direction. It will be easier to keep track of where your next needle and thread pass should be. (Left-handed beaders often find it easier to work always in an anticlockwise direction.) The trick is to be consistent in whichever direction you work the piece.

— Component 4
— Component 5

— Component 1

— Component 3
— Component 2

Tools & Materials

- 25 g size 8 Gilt-lined Medium Lilac Opal (**A**)

- 5 g size 11 opaque brown rainbow seed beads (**B**)

- 30 x 3 mm AB purple fire-polished beads (**C**)

- 0.5 g size 15 opaque brown rainbow seed beads (**D**)

- Fireline (0.12 mm) or nylon beading thread
- Conditioning wax
- Scissors
- Size 12 beading needle

Length (including fastening): 20.5 cm (7¾ in)

Width: 1.5 cm (⅝ in)

TIP
Don't worry that your beads look nothing like the diagrams for the first 3 rows. As you step up for Row 4 the work will take shape, with the skipped beads from Row 2 slipping in to form the bottom row of beads shown in fig. 4.

COMPONENT 1: MAIN BRACELET CUFF BASE

Row 1
a) Thread 90 cm (36 in) of conditioned thread on to a needle.
b) Thread 16A on to thread, leaving a 15-cm (6-in) tail.
c) Working clockwise, form the beads into a ring by passing the needle back through the first 4 beads (**fig. 1**, beads 1–4).

Row 2
Work in modified baseless tubular herringbone stitch (see page 67) as follows:
a) Pick up 2A (**fig. 1**, beads 17 and 18).
b) Pass through the next clockwise bead (**fig. 1**, bead 5).
c) Miss 2 beads (**fig. 1**, beads 6 and 7) and pass through the next clockwise bead (**fig. 1**, bead 8).
d) Working clockwise, place 3 additional pairs of beads around the circle by picking up 2 A beads, passing through 1 bead, missing 2 beads, passing through 1 bead,

etc. until you reach bead 4 again (**fig. 2**).

Step up to the next row
e) Pass the needle up through the next 2 beads (**fig. 3**, bead 4 and bead 17) to step up for row 3.

Row 3
a) Exiting the first bead placed in the last row (**fig. 3**, bead 17) and working clockwise, pick up 1A, 1B and 1A.

ABOUT THE DESIGNER Glenda holds a growing list of awards for her art beadwork, which she also sells on Etsy, as well as writing about beadwork and beyond for various beading magazines.

STEP-BY-STEP DIAGRAMS

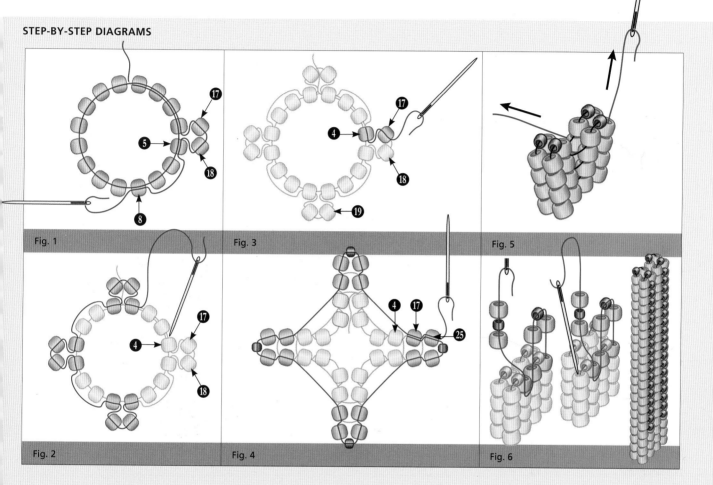

Fig. 1 Fig. 3 Fig. 5
Fig. 2 Fig. 4 Fig. 6

b) Pass down through the next clockwise bead (**fig. 3**, bead 18).
c) Pass up through the next clockwise bead in Row 3 (**fig. 3**, bead 19).
d) Continue stacking 3 beads (1A, 1B and 1A) astride each of the remaining Row 3 pairs.
e) Step up to Row 4 by passing up through the next 2 clockwise beads (**fig. 4**, bead 17 and bead 25).

f) Gently tug on the thread to form the beads into a flattened rectangle (**fig. 5**).

Row 4 onward
a) Exiting the first bead placed in the last row and working clockwise, pick up 1A, 1B and 1A.
b) Pass down through the next clockwise A bead.
c) Pass up through the next

clockwise A bead in Row 3.
d) Continue to stack a set of 3 beads (1A, 1B and 1A) astride each of remaining Row 3 pairs of A beads.
e) Step up to the next row by passing through the next 2 A beads (exiting the first bead placed in this row). See **fig. 6**.
f) Continue to add 1A, 1B, 1A to the stacks of A beads without passing through the B beads, so

that the B beads sit in the ditch in the middle of each stack. Continue in this way until the cuff is the desired length, minus the length of the clasp.

Embellish the herringbone cuff
g) Weave and secure a new thread (approximately 90 cm/ 36 in long) in the cuff.
h) Position the needle and thread to exit a size 11 bead on the left-

DESIGNER: GLENDA MAC NAUGHTON

hand side at one end of the cuff, with your needle and thread pointing to the centre of the cuff (**fig. 7**).

i) Pick up 2B, 1C and 2B.

j) Pass through the corresponding B bead on the right-hand side of the cuff.

k) Pick up 2B, pass back through the C bead, pick up 2B and pass back through the left-hand B bead.

l) Pull gently but firmly on the needle and thread to create a small X-shaped embellishment on the top of the herringbone base (**fig. 8**). Pass the needle down 2 A beads on the left-hand side and out of the next B, ready to place the next embellishment.

Note: If the embellishment sits too loosely on the cuff, use 1B instead of 2B in steps 9 and 11.

m) Following steps 8–12, place as many of these X-shaped embellishments as you desire.

COMPONENT 2: PEYOTE BAR FOR THE TOGGLE CLOSURE

a) Using B beads, work 10 rows of a 12-bead-wide flat peyote-stitch strip (see page 73).

b) Zip the flat peyote stitch band into a tube (see page 103).

c) Add end beads to the tube as follows:

Pass through the tube and pick

TIP

Practise making the square shape on page 112 before tackling the rectangular toggle to familiarise yourself with the peyote and herringbone stitch combinations.

up 1A and 1B, and pass back through the A bead and the centre of the peyote tube. Repeat this step. Reinforce these end embellishments by passing through each of them twice more. Secure and cut your thread. See **fig. 9** for completed bar with end beads.

COMPONENT 3: HERRINGBONE STRAP TO ZIP CUFF TO THE BAR OF THE TOGGLE

a) Position the needle and thread to exit a central A bead at one

end of the cuff (**fig. 10**).

NB: ensure you have at least 20 cm (8 in) of working thread available.

b) Work 18 rows of flat herringbone stitch, using B beads off the 2 central A beads.

c) Join the end of the strip to the matching 2A beads on the underside of the cuff (**fig. 11**).

d) Zip the middle of the flat herringbone strip to the 2 middle beads of the peyote bar tube (**fig. 12**). Reinforce this join carefully, secure your thread and then cut it.

COMPONENT 4: RECTANGULAR PEYOTE AND HERRINGBONE TOGGLE

Create 2 flat rectangles and zip them up to form the rectangular toggle closure.

To create the flat rectangles, work a modified form of circular peyote as follows:

Side 1, Row 1

a) Thread 36B.

b) Form into a circle as per component 1, row 1 (see page 142).

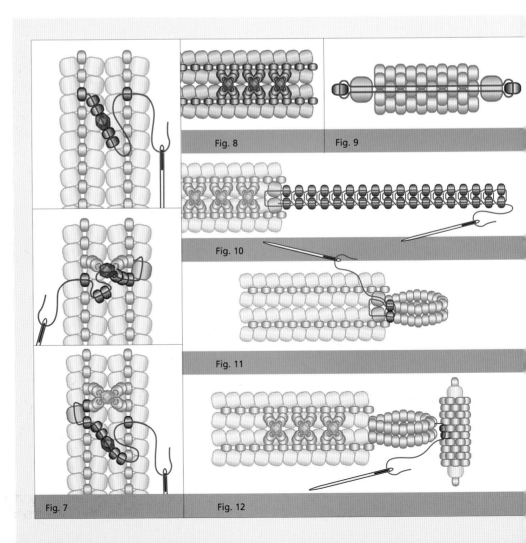

Fig. 7

Fig. 8

Fig. 9

Fig. 10

Fig. 11

Fig. 12

Row 2

Start at the bead marked 'X'. Inner and outer dark beads are added last.

a) Pick up 2B and pass through the next bead.

b) Pick up 1B, miss a bead and pass through the next bead. Repeat once more (short side).

c) Pick up 2B and pass through the next bead.

d) Pick up 1B, miss a bead and pass through the next bead. Repeat 4 more times (long side).

e) Repeat Row 2 steps 1–4.

Row 3

a) Step up to the next row. (This will be Row 4 in **fig. 13a**, as Rows

1 and 2 form the first 3 rows of the toggle.)

b) Follow the graph in **fig. 13a** to complete Rows 1–5, the outer row, and then weave through to the inner side of the rectangle to complete the inner row.

Side 2

a) Follow Row 1 and Row 2 instructions for Side 1, omitting the inner and outer rows.

b) Zip Sides 1 and 2 together, using the inner and outer rows as joining beads.

Embellish herringbone toggle with a 3-bead picot

c) Position the needle and thread

to exit a Row 3 bead near the herringbone corners of the toggle (**fig. 14**).

d) Pick up 1D, 1C, and 1D and pass through the equivalent bead on the other side of the herringbone corner (**fig. 14**).

COMPONENT 5: BEAD HERRINGBONE STRAP TO SECURE TOGGLE TO CUFF

a) At the opposite end of the cuff, repeat Component 3 Steps 2–3 (**fig. 10**).

b) Position the rectangular toggle over the strip and then complete Component 3 Step 4 to secure it to the cuff (**fig. 15**).

c) Secure and cut any loose working threads.

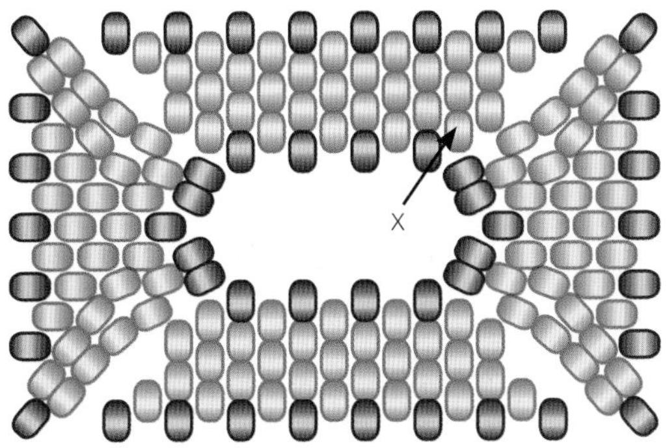

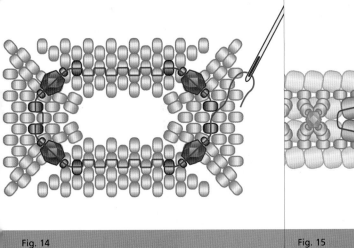

Side 1

Fig. 13a

Side 2

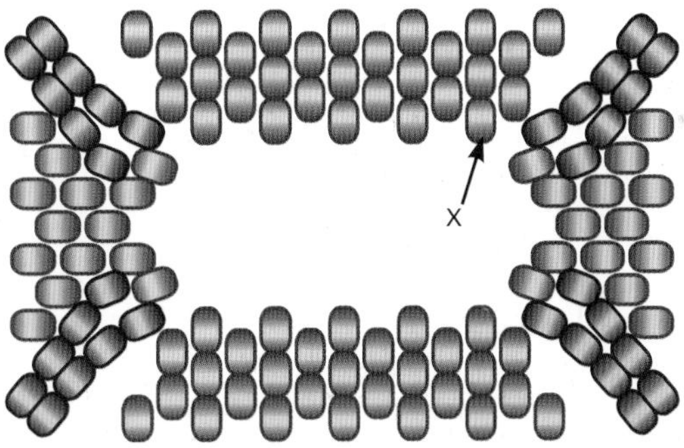

Fig. 13b

Fig. 14

Fig. 15

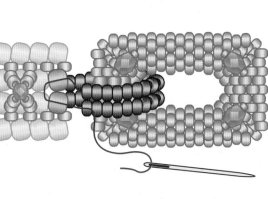

DESIGNER: KERRIE SLADE

Herringbone Harmony Necklace

If you like your beadwork to be in perfect harmony, take a little extra time and work one half of the rope clockwise and the other half anticlockwise so that they form a mirror image of each other. Then join them seamlessly into a herringbone tube to form a smoothly elegant flower.

Tools & Materials

- Approximately 15 g size 11 seed beads (**A**)

- Approximately 5 g size 15 seed beads (**B**)

- 7 x 6 mm Swarovski crystal pearls (**C**)

- Beading thread to match your chosen beads
- Scissors
- Conditioning wax
- Size 10 to 12 beading needles
- Clasp
- 2 jump rings
- Chain-nose pliers

TIP
Try making just the flower as a pendant: starting with a ladder-stitched ring of 4 beads, work a row of herringbone followed by an increase and then follow steps 2 to 9 of 'To join the ropes and make the flower'.

Necklace length: 46 cm (18 in)
Flower length: 4.5 cm (1¾ in)

ABOUT THE DESIGNER Kerrie has 'lived and breathed beads' since her first encounter with beading around ten years ago. She runs her own beading company where she showcases her creations, sells her patterns and runs tutorials.

FIRST HALF OF THE NECKLACE

Step 1 Thread your needle with a comfortable length of conditioned thread (you will need to add new lengths of thread as required). Leaving a 40-cm (16-in) tail, ladder stitch 4A into a row (**fig. 1**).

Step 2 Join the beads into a ring by ladder stitching the first and last beads together (**fig. 2**).

Step 3 Working in a clockwise direction, begin tubular herringbone stitch by picking up 2A and passing your needle down the next bead in the previous row and up the next bead. Pick up 2A and pass your needle down the next bead in the previous row and up the next bead. Complete the row by stepping up through the first bead of this row – 2 beads (**fig. 3**).

Step 4 Repeat step 3 twice more until you have a total of 4 rows, including the original ladder-stitch row. Pull your thread tightly as you work and encourage your work to form a narrow tube (**fig. 4**).

Step 5 Switch to twisted tubular herringbone stitch by repeating step 3 but completing the row with a step up through the beads in the previous 3 rows together with the first bead of this row – a total of 4 beads instead of 2 (**fig. 5**).

Step 6 Repeat step 5 (adding 4 beads in each row and finishing by stepping up through 4 beads) until the first half of your rope is the desired length (approximately 20 cm/8 in for a 46-cm/18-in finished length). Add new lengths of thread as required. Do not weave in the last working thread at the end (**fig. 6**). The twist in the 2 stacks, with 1 higher than the other, will begin to show after 7 or 8 rows.

Add on bead loop for clasp

Step 7 Go back to the beginning of the twisted tube and, using the tail thread, ladder stitch 15 pairs of A beads to 1 half of the ladder stitched in step 1 (**fig. 7**).

Step 8 Ladder stitch the final pair of beads added in the previous step to the free pair of beads in the ladder stitched in step 1, to form a loop. Pass your needle through both pairs of beads several times to secure. Tie off and trim this thread only (**fig. 8**).

STEP-BY-STEP DIAGRAMS

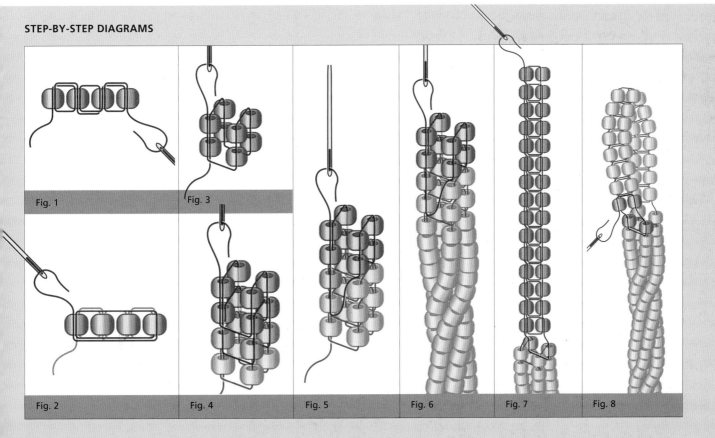

Fig. 1

Fig. 2

Fig. 3

Fig. 4

Fig. 5

Fig. 6

Fig. 7

Fig. 8

DESIGNER: KERRIE SLADE

SECOND HALF OF THE NECKLACE

Step 1 Follow steps 1 to 8 to create a second length of rope, but work in an anticlockwise direction. Make sure that both halves of your rope are exactly the same length (**fig. 9**).

TO JOIN THE ROPES AND MAKE THE FLOWER (WORKED ANTICLOCKWISE)

Step 1 Hold your work so that the 2 sections of rope are parallel, with the taller stacks on the outer edges, your working thread from the left-hand rope exiting the bottom-right stack and a tail thread exiting the bottom-left stack of the right-hand rope. Using the working thread, join the 2 sections together by working a row of herringbone stitch using all 4 stacks (this is an 8-bead row) and complete the row by stepping up through the first bead of the row (**fig. 10**).

Step 2 Work another row of herringbone using the 4 new stacks (this is an 8-bead row) and complete the row by stepping up through the first bead of this row (**fig. 11**).

Step 3 Begin an increase row by adding 2A to each stack and 1B between each stack (this is a 12-bead row) and complete the row by stepping up through the first bead of the row (**fig. 12**).

Step 4 Complete the increase by working a second row, adding 2A to each stack and 2B between each stack (this is a 16-bead row) and complete the row by stepping up through the first bead of the row (**fig. 13**).

Step 5 Treat the pair of B beads added in the previous step as new stacks and work 22 rows of tubular herringbone stitch, adding 2A to each A bead stack and 2B to each B bead stack (each row is a 16-bead row). Complete each row by stepping up through the first bead of the row.

Step 6 Still adding A beads to the A bead stacks and B beads to the B bead stacks, work another row of herringbone – but for each stitch, pass your needle down 2 beads and up 2 beads instead of 1. (3 beads including new ones.) Complete the row by stepping up through 2 beads and the first bead of the row (**fig. 14**).

Step 7 Repeat step 6, but for each stitch pass your needle down 3 beads and up 3 beads instead of 1 (4 beads including new ones) and complete the row by stepping up through 3 beads and the first bead of the row (**fig. 15**).

Step 8 Add a picot of 3A to each A bead stack and a picot of 3B beads to each B bead stack and pass your needle down 4 beads and up 4 beads. Complete the row by stepping up through 4 beads and the first 2 beads of the row (**fig. 16**).

Step 9 To add the 'stamen' to your flower, use either the working thread or a tail thread and travel until your needle is exiting a bead at the beginning of the flower tube. Pass your needle down inside the tube. Pick up 7C and 1A and pass your needle back through the C beads and exit another A bead at the top of the flower. Travel through all of the new beads one more time to reinforce the stamen and pass your needle through another A bead at the top of the flower. Tie off and trim all remaining threads (**fig. 17**).

Step 10 Using your chain-nose pliers, attach a jump ring and clasp to the beaded loops at the ends of your ropes.

Fig. 9

Fig. 10

Fig. 11

Fig. 12

Fig. 13

Fig. 14

Fig. 15

Fig. 16

Fig. 17

DESIGNER: CAROL DEAN SHARPE

Mixed Linx Bracelet

This is a three-drop, even-count peyote bracelet using only three colours of size 11 cylinder beads. Made with cylinder beads, it is just under 2.5 cm (1 in) wide. You can make it wider by substituting size 10 (or even size 8) cylinder beads or make it narrower by switching to size 15 cylinder beads. Don't feel limited to using the colours in the example, either (see opposite).

Length: 20 cm (8 in)
Width: 2 cm (¾ in)

Tools & Materials

- 724 x Palladium Plated cylinder beads (**A**)
- 650 x Bright Gold 24 ct Plated cylinder beads (**B**)
- 552 x Gunmetal cylinder beads (**C**)
- Braided monofilament beading thread
- Size 12 beading needle
- 6 mm gold-plated magnetic clasp (or any clasp of your choice)
- Jump rings
- Chain-nose pliers

Step 1 Thread the needle and cut a comfortable working length of beading thread and pick up the following beads: 1A, 3C, 2A, 8B and 4C for a total of 18 beads (not counting your stop bead if you are using one) (**fig. 1**). This will be transformed into your first 2 rows of beading in step 2.

Step 2 (**fig. 2a–2c**) Pick up 1C and 2A, skip the last 3 beads you picked up in Step 1 and pass through the next 3 beads. Pick up 3B, skip 3 beads and pass through the next 3B beads. Pick up 3B, skip 3 beads and pass through the last 3 beads. You have now completed the first 3 rows of your bracelet.

Step 3 Pick up 2A, and 1C, skip 3 beads and pass through the next 3 beads. Pick up 3B, skip 3 beads and pass through the next 3 beads. Pick up 3B, skip 3 beads and pass through the last 3 beads. Continue to follow the chart in the chart in **fig. 3**, reading from top left to bottom right.

Step 4 With your thread now emerging from the A bead as indicated in **fig. 3**, keep beading until you have reached the length you prefer less the length added by whatever clasp you choose.

Step 5 With a new length of thread, attach 1 half of the clasp to each end (**fig. 4**). Retrace your thread path several times.

TIP

Getting the tension right in three-drop peyote is a little like Goldilocks finding the perfect bed. I suggest making a few practice swatches before starting on the actual bracelet. I place the thumb and middle finger on either side of the beads I have just added before drawing my thread completely through. This allows me to get a good fit between bead columns while preventing my beads from buckling up due to too much tension.

Carol Dean is a former English teacher and professional writer/editor
who founded Sand Fibers, her jewellery and design company, in 2005
and hasn't looked back since.

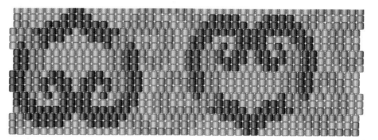

While I've indulged in my personal
love of mixed metals, this piece would
be equally fun in red and pink.

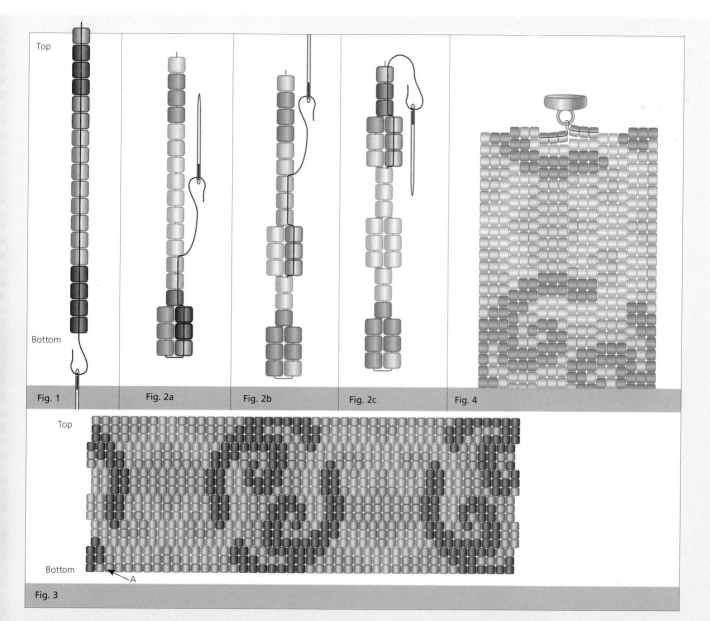

Top

Bottom

Fig. 1

Fig. 2a

Fig. 2b

Fig. 2c

Fig. 4

Top

Bottom

A

Fig. 3

Glossary

2-drop, 3-drop Picking up and using two or three beads as one bead in a stitch.

Bead soup A seemingly random mix of different-sized seed beads, unified by a colour scheme.

Bezel A ring of beadwork holding a hole-less bead or rivoli in place.

Calottes Also known as clamshells, clamshell crimps, necklace ends, bead tips and knot cups.

Chart A graph paper representation of a bead pattern or picture. Each square represents a bead.

Circle through/circle stitch To pass the needle and thread around and back through the bead you have just passed through.

CRAW Cubic right-angle weave.

Cross bead One bead shared by two rows, usually in netting stitch.

Crystal Glass beads with a small lead content.

Culling Sorting out and discarding broken and misshaped beads.

Decreasing Removing or reducing the number of beads added to narrow or shorten your work.

Dominant hand The hand you use the most (i.e., your right hand if you are right handed).

Figure-of-eight Describing a thread path that forms the shape of a number eight: Across to the right, down to the left, across to the right and back up to the left.

Findings The metal components used to turn beadwork into jewellery.

Focal bead A larger, decorative bead usually centred in a design, or used as one half of a toggle clasp.

Gauge The thickness (diameter) of wire, tigertail or threads.

Half-hitch knot A knot used to anchor the working thread before cutting it or to change the direction of the thread path.

Increasing Adding in extra beads to widen or lengthen your work.

Ladder base A strip of beads worked in ladder stitch, on which to build more beadwork.

Overhand knot A basic knot used to join two thread ends into a loose circle.

Pass through, Pass back through, Pass up through, Pass down through Pass through a bead with threaded needle in the direction indicated by the instruction.

Pick up Use the end of the beading needle to pick up the number of beads indicated, ready to work the next step.

Picot A decorative three-bead edging or point effect.

RAW Right-angle weave.

RAW or CRAW cube A 3D cube consisting of four RAW units.

RAW unit A four-sided flat unit of beads made in RAW.

Rivoli An undrilled (hole-less) faceted crystal bead, rising to a point both front and back, usually but not always backed with a foil.

A selection of rocailles in different sizes and finishes.

Bugle beads, from long to short, straight and twisted.

Rows and rounds To work a row is to stitch beads along the line of the work in hand. A round is to work one circular 'row' of beadwork before stepping up to the next row.

Semiprecious Natural stones and minerals cut or shaped and polished to resemble more expensive gemstones. They usually but not always have drilled holes.

Skip a bead Pass over the bead from the previous row and pass the thread through the next bead along.

Spacer bead A small bead, often metal, used to space out the decorative or focal beads.

Square knot or reef knot Made by tying a left-hand overhand knot and then a right-hand overhand knot. Use to secure a number of strung beads into a ring.

Stack The two-bead-wide column made in herringbone stitch.

Step up To pass the needle through (usually) two beads at the end of a round, ready to work the new round.

Stitch in the ditch Placing a bead in the 'ditch' formed between side-by-side beads, usually in peyote stitch.

Stop bead or tension bead A bead loosely strung at the beginning of the beadwork to hold beads in place for the first few rows.

Tail thread The end of the thread furthest from the needle.

Tension Created by pulling gently or tightly on the beading thread as you work.

Thread path The route the thread follows as it passes through the beads. It will be different for different stitches.

Tumble chips Small, irregular, drilled pieces of semi-precious stone. Usually sold by the strand.

Turn bead The last bead in a sequence, allowing the thread path to change direction.

Weave in the ends To pass the thread back through the beadwork without adding any beads to secure the loose ends.

Wingspan The distance between outstretched arms used to measure lengths of thread.

Working thread The end of thread with the needle attached to it.

Zipping up To close up a strip of peyote stitch by passing the thread through the prominent beads on either end in a zigzag pattern. Like lacing up a corset.

Round glass beads.

A selection of cylinder beads, including double cylinders.

Shapes, Sizes and Quantities

How many beads does it take to make a piece of jewellery?
These tables and guides aim to provide you with some useful
references to help answer such questions.

COMMON BEADS SHAPES

Not all beads are round. They come in
many shapes and sizes. Below are some
of the most common with their names
and how their holes lie:

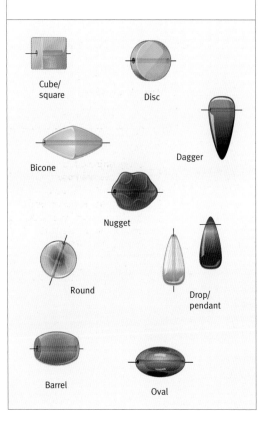

Cube/square

Disc

Bicone

Dagger

Nugget

Round

Drop/pendant

Barrel

Oval

ESTIMATING QUANTITIES

You'll find that the size of beads varies according to manufacturer, finish
on the bead and even colour of the bead. This table shows an average
approximation of bead sizes and a guide to the number needed to
achieve a strung length.

BEAD (APPROXIMATE SIZE)	BEADS PER 2.5 CM (1 IN)	BEADS PER 46 CM (18 IN)	BEADS PER 61 CM (24 IN)
Size 15 seed bead (1.5 mm)	17	307	401
Size 11 seed bead (1.8–2.2 mm)	12–14	210–256	278–339
Size 8 seed bead (3.3 mm)	8	140	185
Size 6 seed bead (4 mm)	6	115	153
2 mm bead	12	230	305
3 mm bead	8	154	203
4 mm bead	6	115	153
5 mm bead	5	92	122
6 mm bead	4	77	102
8 mm bead	3	57	76
10 mm bead	2	46	61
12 mm bead	2	38	51

NECKLACES

The illustration below shows the classic necklace lengths in centimetres and inches, with a guide to where each length sits on the neck and chest. Use these only as a guide; you will need to take measurements when working up your design.

TIP
To determine the correct length of your necklace, drape a tape measure or length of string around your neck so that the centre point sits in the right place on your body and check the measurement.

Choker 36 cm (14 in)

Standard short 40 cm (16 in)

Standard long 46 cm (18–20 in)

Matinee 61 cm (24 in)

Opera 76 cm (30 in)

Long Opera 92 cm (36 in)

Rope 102 cm (40 in)

TIP
Long, unjoined rope necklaces are known as lariats. These look great worn wrapped or knotted around the neck or wrist, in a style that evokes the 1920s.

TABLE OF COMMON SEED BEADS

The table below gives the vital statistics of a number of common bead sizes, providing a conversion chart for the main sizes and the number of beads per gram.

	SEED BEAD SIZE	APPROXIMATE SIZE	NUMBER PER 1 GRAM	NUMBER PER 10 GRAMS	NUMBER PER 100 GRAMS
•	Size 15	1.5 mm	250	2,500	25,000
•	Size 11	1.8–2.2 mm	120	1,200	12,000
•	Size 8	3.3 mm	36	360	3,600
●	Size 6	4 mm	18	180	1,800

CYLINDER BEAD SIZE	APPROXIMATE SIZE	NUMBER PER 1 GRAM	NUMBER PER 10 GRAMS	NUMBER PER 100 GRAMS
Size 11	1.6 mm	200	2,000	20,000

Resources

Suppliers

United States

Beadalon
440 Highland Blvd.,
Coatsville, PA 19320
www.beadalon.com

Beadcats
PO Box 2840,
Wilsonville, OR 97070-2840
+1 (503) 625-2323
www.beadcats.com

Beadin' path, The
15 Main St.,
Freeport,
ME 04032
www.beadinpath.com

Blue Moon Beads
www.bluemoonbeads.com

Cartwright's Sequins
& Vintage Buttons
11108 N. Hwy. 348
Mountainburg, AR 72946
+1 (479) 369-2074
www.ccartwright.com

Charm Factory, Inc.
PO Box 91625,
Albuquerque, NM 87199-1625
+1 (866) 867-5266
www.charmfactory.com

Fire Mountain Gems
One Fire Mountain Way,
Grants Pass, OR 97526-2373
+1 (800) 355-2137
www.firemountaingems.com

FusionBeads.com
+1 (888) 781-3559

Lisa Peters Art
215 Demarest Ave., Closter
NJ 07624
+1 (201) 784-0812
www.lisapetersart.com

Out on a Whim
121 E. Cotati Ave.,
Cotati, CA 94931
+1 (800) 232-3111
www.whimbeads.com

Shipwreck Beads
8560 Commerce Place Dr. NE
Lacey, WA 98516
+1 (800) 950-4232
www.shipwreckbeads.com

Stormcloud Trading Co.
www.beadstorm.com

Thunderbird Supply Company
www.thunderbirdsupply.com

United Kingdom

Beads Direct Ltd
10 Duke Street
Loughborough
Leicestershire
LE11 1ED
United Kingdom
+44 (0)1509 218028
www.beadsdirect.co.uk

The Bead Cellar
Broad Street,
Black Torrington,
Devon,
EX21 5PT
+44 (0)1409 231442
www.thebeadcellar.co.uk

The Bead Shop Scotland
29 Court Street
Haddington
East Lothian
EH41 3AE
+44 (0)1620 822886
www.beadshopscotland.co.uk

RB Beads
Pacific House Business Centre
Fletcher Way
Carlisle
CA3 0LJ
+44 (0)1228 406360
www.rbbeads.co.uk

Westcoast
Pam Gordon
6 Mill Rise
Helsby, Frodsham
WA6 0PL
+44 (0)1928 890448
www.westcoastgemsandbeads.
com

France

Perles & Co
25, rue Henri Moissan
81000 Albi
France
+33 (0)825 120 336
www.perlesandco.co.uk

Online Resources

thebeadedmolecules.blogspot.
co.uk
A blog exploring the similarities
between molecule structures and
beaded beads.

www.beadinfinitum.com
Taking the mathematical
approach to making complex,
beautiful spheres and other
beaded beads.

www.youtube.com/
watch?v=P1Ib0qsQSy4
Heather Collin's excellent CRAW
video tutorial.

abeadstore.com
A selection of simple beading
projects, tips, FAQs and a
retail area.

www.auntiesbeads.com
Online retailer with a wide range
of beads and findings as well as
resources for weekly projects and
video tutorials.

www.beadersshowcase.com
An online community with a
place to showcase your work and
chat to other members.

www.beadingdaily.com
Site containing projects,
information, contests, galleries
and chat.

www.beadingtimes.com
Excellent source of information
on all aspects of jewellery design.
Updated monthly.

www.beadmagazine.co.uk
Site with projects, galleries and
forums. Also Bead TV, showing
tutorials, workshops and
demonstrations.

www.beadwork.about.com
A site with an active forum and
lots of links and articles.

www.beadworkersguild.org.uk
A membership site publishing a
journal and a selection of books,
as well as running workshops
and beading events.

www.etsy.com
A social commerce website
focused on handmade and
vintage items as well as art and
craft supplies.

www.firemountain.com
Online retailer with a huge range
of gemstones and other supplies
as well as an 'encycloBEADia',
gallery and tutorials section.

www.jewelinfo4u.com
A vast source of information
ranging from gemstone data to
tools required for jewellery
making and designer galleries.

www.merchantsoverseas.com
Information on all things
Swarovski, with colour, shape
and size charts, seasonal colour
trends and an online retail area.

Magazines

Bead Magazine
Bead UK
Park Farm, Arundel,
West Sussex, BN18 0AG
T: +44 (0) 1903 884988
E: support@ashdown.co.uk
www.beadmagazine.co.uk

Bead and Button
www.beadandbutton.com
A magazine packed with loads
of projects to challenge and
inspire readers of all interests
and abilities.

Beadwork Magazine
www.beadingdaily.com

Societies

United States
There are bead societies in most US states – just contact your local library for details. Alternatively, a quick internet search will produce a list of possible societies and groups.

Austin Bead Society
P.O. Box 656
Austin, TX 78767-0656
Email: austinbeadsociety@yahoo.com
www.austinbeadsociety.org

Baltimore Bead Society
8510 High Ridge Road
Ellicott City, MD 21043
Email: baltbead@bcpl.net
www.baltobead.org

Bead Society of Greater Chicago
P.O. Box 8103
Wilmette, IL 60091-8103
www.bsgc.org

Bead Society of Greater New York, The
P.O. Box 6219
FDR Station
New York, NY 10150
Email: info@nybead.org
http://nybead.org

Bead Society of Greater Washington, The
The Jenifer Building, Ground Floor
400 Seventh Street Northwest
Washington, DC 20004
Email: info@beadmuseumdc.org
www.bsgw.org

Bead Society of New Hampshire, The
P.O. Box 356
Atkinson, NH 03811
Email: beadsocietynh@yahoo.com
www.nebeads.com/BSNH

Bead Society of Orange County, The
2002 N. Main Street
Santa Ana, CA 92706
www.beadsocietyoc.org
Upper Midwest Bead Society
3000 University Avenue SE, #5
Minneapolis, MN 55414

Cumberland Valley Bead Society
Box 41903
Nashville, TN 37204
Email: johnsoncaren@hotmail.com
www.cvbeads.net

Great Lakes Beadworkers Guild
P.O. Box 1639
Royal Oak, MI 48068-1639
www.greatlakesbeadworkersguild.org

International Society of Glass Beadmakers
1120 Chester Avenue #470
Cleveland, OH 44114
www.isgb.org

Los Angeles Bead Society, The
PO Box 241874
Culver City
CA 90024–9674

Madison Bead Society
P.O. Box 620383
Middleton, WI 53562-0383
Email: madisonbeadsoc@hotmail.com
www.madisonbeadsociety.org

Northwest Bead Society
P.M.B. 564
4603 N.E. University Village
Seattle, WA 98105
www.nwbeadsociety.org

Oklahoma Bead Society
Teresa Davis, Librarian
5144 S New Haven Ave.
Tulsa, OK 74135
Email: teresadavis50@hotmail.com
www.okbeadsociety.com

Portland Bead Society
P.O. Box 997
Portland, OR 97207-0997
www.beadport.com

Rocky Mountain Bead Society (RMBS)
P.O. Box 480721
Denver, CO 80248-0721
Email: rmbs@rockybeads.org
www.rockybeads.org

San Antonio Bead and Ornament Society
Email: sabostx@hotmail.com
www.homestead.com/sabostx/

South Jersey Bead Society
53 Sunset Drive
Voorhees, NJ 08043-4941
Email: prancingpixel@yahoo.com
www.southjerseybeadsociety.org

Wyoming TumbleBeaders Bead Society
P.O. Box 1431
Cheyenne, WY 82003-1431
www.geocities.com/wyotumblebeaders/

United Kingdom
The Bead Society of Great Britain
1 Casburn Lane, Burwell,
Cambridgeshire CB25 OED
www.beadsociety.org.uk/

Glass Beadmakers UK – Showcasing the work of glass beadmakers
6 Scrap Villas,
Hastingwood Road,
Hastingwood,
Essex,
CM17 9JX
www.gbuk.org

UK Beaders – an online beading community
www.uk-beaders.co.uk/

Beading in London – site run by Jean Power for all things beady in the UK's capital.
www.beadinginlondon.co.uk/

Beads & Beyond
Traplet Publications Ltd
Traplet House
Pendragon Close
Malvern
WR14 1GA
General Enquiries: +44(0)1684 588500
Email: hello@traplet.com
www.beadsandbeyondmagazine.com

Index

Acknowledgements

- p.10bl/bl, Poston, David, www.davidposton.net
- p.10–11c, Kaiser, Ulli, www.ullikaiser.co.uk
- pp.11t, 14b, 16t, 122t, Reid, Caron, www.caronmichelle.com
- pp.12t, 14c, 15b, 41c, 52c, 64–65tc, 104t, Airs, Jennifer, www.jdjewellery.co.uk
- pp.12c, 78t, 110, Glasser, Julie, www.julieglasser.com
- pp.12b, 15t, 17t, 92tl, Tang-Lim, Helena, www.manek-manek.com
- pp.13c/ b, 17c, 40t, 54tr, 60b, 98tr, Davy, Lynn, http://lynndavybeadwork.co.uk
- p.16b, Poupazis, Joy, www.cjpoupazis.com
- pp.16c, 17b, 41t, Wiseman, Jill, www.tapestrybeads.com
- p.30b MIYUKI Co., www.miyuki-beads.co.jp
- p.40b, 72t, VanPelt, Natasha, Morita of Inspirational Beading http://inspirationalbeading.blogspot.co.uk
- p.54tl, Hamill, Michelle, www.pardalote.net
- p.84tr, Tucker, Sarah, http://sarahtuckerbeadwork.weebly.com
- p.116t, Amybeads, http://amybeads.blogspot.com
- p.132–137, Dale, Nancy, www.nedbeads.com
- p.138–141, Collin, Heather
- p.142–145, MacNaughton, Glenda
- p.146–149, Slade, Kerrie, www.kerrieslade.co.uk
- p.150–151, Sharpe, Carol Dean

The earrings shown on page 39bl were inspired by the Volcanoes Necklace featured in *Sabine Lippert's Beaded Fantasies*, published by Lark Crafts 2012.

p. 39br: Glazed stoneware bowl:
Marion Hurley mazzo22@hotmail.co.uk

The projects on pages 62–63 and 129 were designed by Mary Marshall: Mary has loved beads since childhood, when she received a tiny glass vial of rocailles as a gift. She loves to make unsupported beaded beads and enjoys all types of beading, especially while listening to films she's seen dozens of times before.

The project featured on page 120–121 was designed by Karen Wilkinson: Karen Wilkinson is a self-taught jewellery designer. She took jewellery up as a hobby after the birth of her second daughter and was soon addicted to beads! Karen has dabbled with many crafts over the years including polymer clay, beadweaving and pearl knotting. Her work can be seen on her website: www.trinity-jewellery.co.uk

Author acknowledgements
My beading life began at a spiral stitch workshop run by my friend and former boss, Jo Lochhead. Without that introduction, this book would not exist. Nor would it have happened if the lovely Mary Marshall had not been there to provide practical help and moral support. I had huge help and support from the fine team at Quarto, whose brilliant idea this book was. My thanks to all of you.